SIX CANADIAN PLAYS

BABEL RAP
John Lazarus

*

HEDGES
Dave Carley

*

HEROES
Ken Mitchell

*

MOON PEOPLE
Aviva Ravel

*

HURRAY FOR JOHNNY CANUCK
Ken Gass

*

THE KOMAGATA MARU INCIDENT
Sharon Pollock

Playwrights Canada Press
Toronto

Six Canadian Plays © Copyright
PLAYWRIGHTS CANADA PRESS 1992
Babel Rap © John Lazarus 1972.
Hedges © Dave Carley 1985
Heroes © Ken Mitchell 1971.
Moon People © Aviva Ravel 1988.
Hurray for Johnny Canuck © Ken Gass 1975
The Komagata Maru Incident © Sharon Pollock 1978

PLAYWRIGHTS CANADA PRESS is the publishing imprint of Playwrights Union of Canada, 54 Wolseley Street, 2nd Floor Toronto, Ontario Canada M5T 1A5 Tel: (416) 947-0201 Fax: (416) 947-0159

PLAYWRIGHTS CANADA PRESS operates with generous assistance from The Canada Council, the Ontario Arts Council, and the Ontario Ministry of Culture and Communications.

Front cover design by Tony Hamill & David Caron.
Book designed and edited by Tony Hamill.

Canadian Cataloguing in Publication Data

Main entry under title: Six Canadian Plays   ISBN 0-88754-469-X
1. Canadian drama (English) - 20th century.*   I. Hamill, Tony - ed.

PS8315.S58 1991   C812'.5408   C91-094472-5
PR9196.6.S58 1991

First edition: March 1992.
Printed and bound in Canada by Best Gagne.

TABLE OF CONTENTS

∞

Printed in Canada on acid-free paper

Printed on paper
containing over 50%
recycled paper including
10% post-consumer fibre.

INTRODUCTION

What is a Canadian play? The question is asked so often that most playwrights are tired of hearing it. It goes without saying that Canadian plays do not necessarily take place in a Canadian setting, nor are they necessarily bedecked with beavers, maple leaves, or prairie farmhouses, any more than Shakespeare's plays are limited to English subjects or locales.

All artists are influenced by the environment in which they live and one need only travel to the United States or further abroad to know that Canadians *are* different despite the fact our language is shared by people of many other countries. A subtle difference pervades our work, even when it deals with legends from other lands.

In looking through this collection of Canadian plays, I'm struck by the number of times the notion of "hero" comes up, and how this theme is shaded by the Canadian sensibilities of the writer. Ken Mitchell's play *Heroes* concerns itself with a re-evaluation of four well-known comic book personalities and examines them in a new, realistic light. The play is harsh and satiric, and suggests that heroes, and perhaps even heroism, are fading notions in today's commercial world. *Hurray for Johnny Canuck* appears to offer the opposite viewpoint in its nostalgic glorification of Canadian comic-book heroes of the past, but there is satire here as well, plus the ironic counterpoint of a real-life Canadian reacting to Canuck's fantasy adventures.

One might argue that the character Hopkinson, from *The Komagata Maru Incident* is a modern tragic hero, caught in a complex web of social and political consequences that ultimately lead to his death. It is clear, however, that playwright Sharon Pollock is also writing an indictment of a shameful chapter in Canadian history, wherein the real heroes are offstage, victims stranded off the shores of an inhospitable and racist society. In Dave Carley's *Hedges* we find the same issue but in a much lighter vein. In this wildly comic parable, a variation on the good-fences/good-neighbours theme, the Smiths and Joneses take their intolerance for each others' eccentricities to the point of absurdity.

In *Moon People*, by Aviva Ravel, we are confronted with a contemporary "anti-hero", in this case a fiercely rebellious "anti-herione" named Harriet. Harriet, a 17-year social misfit, struggles to regain her dignity by assaulting a well-established actress who, she believes, is responsible for the horrors of her childhood. Finally, there is John Lazarus' *Bable Rap*, in which the two central characters are presented in the ironic tradition familiar to a good deal of modern drama. Worker and Smoker are little heroes who battle forces greater than themselves. Their accomplishments appear small, but the realization they come to is intensely meaningful in terms of their own lives.

While these plays have similarities in theme, they provide considerable variety of theatrical style. They range from the realistic approach of *Moon People* to the absurdist *Hedges* and *Babel Rap*. There is also the zany cartoon style of *Hurray for Johnny Canuck*, as well as the hybrid cartoon-realism of *Heroes*. While the scenes of *The Komagata Maru Incident* have the keen edge of documentary realism, the play is framed in an imaginative carnival-barker theatricality.

Above all, the boldness of the writing in these plays begs for live performances, and, hopefully, they will provide exciting vehicles for the imagination of young actors. The plays are all deeply imbued with a Canadian sensibility, and it is perhaps this as much as anything that has made them so successful with Canadian audiences.

Ken Gass

EDITOR'S FOREWORD

Success with audiences, as playwright Ken Gass indicates in his introduction to this collection, is the primary reason for publishing *Six Canadian Plays*. This book is actually an updated and reformatted version of our most popular book ever -- *Five Canadian Plays*.

After numerous reprints, *Five Canadian Plays* went out of print for a short while, but some of the plays in the collection continued to sell individually in large numbers, especially to high schools and theatres. When we decided to reprint, we chose the three most popular plays in the original book -- *Babel Rap, Heroes,* and *Hurray for Johnny Canuck* -- and matched them with three new short plays with similar themes which had also proven their success with audiences and students of Drama and English -- *Hedges, Moon People,* and *The Komagata Maru Incident*.

The continued success of all six plays is based on their ability to mirror our society -- to show us something of ourselves that we recognize. Whether we like this reflection or not, these plays make us stop and take a careful look at who we are and where we came from. The plays reflect both our personal and collective values -- at the turn of the century, during World War II, and right now. The plays also question whether these values have changed for better or worse, or remained the same. Do we learn from our mistakes; do we improve as people and as a society, or do we just pretend that we do and turn a blind eye to our own faults? Are we heroes, or anti-heroes, or simply human beings -- a bit of both.

As you read and perform these plays, we hope you learn something wonderful about yourself and about this wonderful country.

Tony Hamill

BABEL RAP

JOHN LAZARUS

John was born in 1947 in Montreal. He studied acting at the National Theatre School, and worked as an actor, radio copywriter, and critic, before becoming a playwright and screenwriter. His plays include *Dreaming and Duelling* (a collaboration), *The Late Blumer, Village of Idiots, Genuine Fakes, David for Queen, Homework & Curtains, Medea's Disgust,* and the *"Binnie Plays"* for children: *Schoolyard Games, Not So Dumb, Night Light,* and *Dirty Secrets.* John also writes for film and television, and teaches playwriting at Studio 58. He lives in Vancouver.

AUTHOR'S INTRODUCTION

In 1972, I was a young hippie actor with playwriting ambitions, working with a tiny theatre troupe called Troupe. We were planning an evening of one-acts. I told myself (wrongly) that if I was a real playwright I should be able to write a play about the very next thing I saw and I looked up and saw the lighting man's stepladder. So I decided to write a play that my friend Alex and I could perform **on** a stepladder, which would represent the biggest structure in the world. And I went home that night and wrote *Babel Rap*.

Nowadays, *Babel Rap* reads very much like a kid's first play, which is what it was. I've been tempted to do rewrites on it, but I've decided to let it stand as written. It is now older than my adult daughter. Some day it will be older than me. It will not go away. Students just keep doing it. I have nightmares where I'm winning the Nobel Prize, and the King of Sweden leans over and whispers, "We're giving you this because I did Babel Rap in high school."

John Lazarus

BABEL RAP

Babel Rap looks at the biblical story of the building of the Tower of Babel from the viewpoint of two very ordinary workmen. The comic decision as to who should smoke and who should hammer is quite ironic when set against the pretentious design of the tower itself. The workmen's suppositions regarding the Almighty, and how their work fits into the Scheme of Things is classic comic subject matter. The playwright has constructed a unique situation for exploring these philosophical preoccupations in an amusing way.

Much of the production value stems from the nature of the exchanges between the two central characters: even while taking themselves seriously they have remarkable insight into the absurdity of their situation. The play requires very little in the way of sets and props since most of the attention is focussed on the workmen, but it provides an opportunity for skillful stage business and comic interplay as long as the serious concerns of the characters are never lost.

The final absurd jumble of dialogue brings to an hilarious climax the desperate struggle of two men to remain rational in the midst of a mad universe.

Babel Rap was first produced by Troupe of Vancouver in April 1972, with the following cast:

A WORKER   *John Lazarus*

A SMOKER   *Alexander Diakun*

Directed by John Lazarus.

A revised version was produced in March 1975 for the opening of Citadel II in Edmonton with the following cast:

A WORKER   *Alan Lysell*

A SMOKER   *Scott Swan*

Alan Lysell and *Scott Swan* made very important contributions to the revisions, for which the author extends deep thanks.

THE CHARACTERS

A WORKER

A SMOKER

The characters do not have to be male, of course.

THE COSTUMES

Modern dress is recommended - overalls or work clothes, with touches of colour about them. Biblical robes are acceptable too: one production had the actors in robes, sandals, and MacMillan-Bloedel hardhats.

THE SET

The highest point on the Tower of Babel. The original production took place on a step-ladder, built for the purpose, that was meant to represent the top of the tower. Whatever the set design, it should be established early on that the stage floor is accepted as nonexistent - that is, the actors look down through infinite space, and never touch the floor. We have found that the best production design has been the simplest. A sky-cloth backdrop or cyclorama is also recommended, maybe even a cloud or two.

BABEL RAP

The sound of hammering in darkness. Lights up. The WORKER *is busy hammering, working on the tower. The* SMOKER *is relaxing with a cigarette, watching the birds fly by below. After a few moments, the noise of the hammering begins to bother the* SMOKER. *He raps briskly on the side of the tower like an annoyed tenant. The* WORKER *repeats the brisk pattern, deafeningly, with his hammer.*

SMOKER   Hey, would you like to stop and have a smoke?

WORKER   *(stops hammering; short pause, pointedly)* No thanks. I'm working.

SMOKER   *(pointedly)* Oh. *(returning to his smoking and watching the birds)*

> *The* WORKER *looks at him, and goes back to hammering. After a moment, the noise bothers the* SMOKER.

SMOKER   Listen, do you mind? *(as the* WORKER *stops)* I'm trying to relax here. Have my cigarette and watch the birds. I find that hammering distracting.

WORKER   Yeah?

SMOKER   Yeah.

WORKER   I'm working my ass off, and you're sitting on yours, and you find my hammering distracting?

SMOKER   Yeah!

Pause.

WORKER What about all that goddamn noise you're making? All that sucking and blowing. *(noisily imitating a drag on a cigarette)* That's what I call distracting.

SMOKER Yeah?

WORKER Yeah. Also the smoke from your cigarette is irritating my sensitive nostrils.

SMOKER Yeah?

WORKER Yeah! *(pausing)* Look, we're at a very high altitude. The atmosphere is thin. The smoke is proportionately more irritating.

SMOKER All right, whaddaya wanna do? *(pausing)*

WORKER Why don't we both work hard for five minutes and then stop for a smoke?

SMOKER Why don't we both smoke hard for five minutes and then go back to work?

Pause, both thinking.

BOTH Okay...

WORKER I'll work for five minutes...

SMOKER I'll smoke for five minutes...

BOTH And then we'll both take a break!

WORKER No smoking!

SMOKER No hammering!

WORKER Shalom! *(simultaneously)*

SMOKER Shazam! *(simultaneously)*

> *The* WORKER *resumes hammering.*
> *The* SMOKER *puffs thoughtfully.*

SMOKER *(amiably)* You know, it's fortunate that we get along as well as we do.

WORKER *(stops hammering, chuckling)* Yes, isn't it. Considering how high up we are!

> *They chuckle.*

SMOKER And considering why we're here.

WORKER Mmm... Not everybody gets along as well as we do. I'm told there was an incident yesterday on one of the lower parapets. Two workmen pushed each other off the ledge.

SMOKER Really?

WORKER One of them asked for a hammer, and the other one gave him a saw... and in the ensuing dispute, they just pushed each other off the ledge.

SMOKER That seems a bit extreme.

WORKER Yeah, doesn't it. It sounds to me like they had the wrong attitude toward the holy nature of their work.

SMOKER Oh, I don't know about that. They were willing to sacrifice each other for the sake of the Tower. That sounds kind of noble.

WORKER Don't be facetious!

SMOKER I'm not. Those two were probably more successful than we are. Look. Here we've been hammering and sawing since about as far back as I can remember, trying to build this Tower to Heaven.

SMOKER *(continued)* All those guys had to do was get into a bit of a quarrel, and *(indicating a long fall, whistling a descending glissando, followed by a long pan up to Heaven, as he whistles an ascending glissando)* they're probably up in Heaven right now. Looking down upon us and giggling.

WORKER *(working cheerfully)* That never occurred to me! This Tower's been my whole life! Whaddaya know.

SMOKER Well, don't let it worry you.

WORKER I won't.

SMOKER You know, if you don't mind my saying so, you're probably too involved with the details.You ever ask yourself why we're building this Tower? What's it for?

WORKER To get to Heaven!

SMOKER To get to Heaven.

WORKER What, do you think all this is in vain?

SMOKER Well, we're gonna get to Heaven anyway! When we die! Aren't we?

WORKER Sure! But you have to do something to pass the time before you get there. So why not work on the Tower? It's a good project. Gives people jobs. Makes everybody feel important. And besides, we might succeed! We might get to Heaven any day now!

SMOKER *(uneasily)* Any day now...?

WORKER   Sure! This Tower's a real short-cut! Also, you avoid the pain and inconvenience of dying! *(pausing)* Boy, you really know how to make me feel better about the whole thing. Shalom! *(heartened, returning to his work)*

SMOKER   *(thoughtfully)* Shazam... *(smoking and thinking)* The one thing that keeps bothering me, though...

WORKER   Yeah?

SMOKER   Well, I keep wondering what's going to happen when we get there.

WORKER   *(slowing and stopping work)* How do you mean?

SMOKER   Well, for one thing, how do you know you're there?

WORKER   Well, everybody knows what Heaven is like!

SMOKER   Oh? Really?

WORKER   Sure! There's...blue sky...sunshine...birds singing everywhere...lots of clouds floating around.

SMOKER   Yeah, but there are clouds right here. Some time ago, as a matter of fact, when we were working some stories below, you promised me that when we got above the clouds, we'd be in Heaven.

WORKER   *(shrugging off his former ignorance)* Oh! Well...

SMOKER   Well, we got above the clouds, and what did we find? Clouds.

WORKER   Well, I'm sorry! It's not my fault that this isn't Heaven.

SMOKER   *(pause)* Maybe...Maybe it is.

WORKER   *(horrified)* What?

SMOKER   Sure. This could be Heaven. Blue sky... sunshine... all kinds of clouds drifting by...the occasional bird. Very peaceful.

WORKER   No! No, no, no, no, no! This isn't Heaven!

SMOKER   Why not?

WORKER   Because...well, because Heaven has great golden pillars thrusting up through the clouds, capped with tall spires and vast domes! And long rolling green meadows...and Technicolour gardens, filled with sparkling, jewelled, multi-coloured flowers! And massed chori of angels, singing Beethoven and Handel and Bach! Beautiful angels, everywhere!

They look around, in the direction of the audience.

SMOKER   Nope.

WORKER   Well, it's worth hammering a few nails. *(resuming hammering as the* SMOKER *smokes and thinks)*

SMOKER   Yeah, but...

The WORKER *puts down his hammer with resignation and disgust.*

SMOKER   But I still don't understand what happens when we get there.

WORKER   I'm sorry, but I still don't understand what the hell you're talking about.

SMOKER   Okay, look. We arrive. We look around. We see the angels and the pillars and the gardens of flowers. Hooray! Whoopee! We're in Heaven!

WORKER   Right!

SMOKER   Yeah, well then what? *(pausing)* What do we do
             then? Have lunch? Go sightseeing?...Start
             another tower?

             Pause.

WORKER   Well...we do whatever we want to, I suppose.
             Personally I'd sort of like to just gaze upon the
             countenance of the Almighty.

SMOKER   Yeah...That'd be nice. But you wouldn't want to
             do that forever. For one thing, it'd be rude. You
             don't just walk up to the Almighty and gaze
             upon His countenance, like some gawky tourist.
             You'd want to say something.

WORKER   Well, sure! A private audience with the Almighty
             Himself! Great idea.

SMOKER   What would you say?

WORKER   Well...I'd introduce myself...and I'd introduce
             you...I'd tell Him how happy I was to be there.

SMOKER   Yeah, but He already knows all that. He knows
             who we are. He knows that you're happy to be
             there and that I'm happy to be there.

WORKER   I know. But it's just a way of being polite. You
             know? Making conversation.

SMOKER   Well, maybe He'd take offence.

WORKER   Why should He take offence?

SMOKER   Well, you're sort of talking down to Him, telling
             Him stuff He already knows. What if He says, "I
             already know all that. Tell me something I don't
             already know." Ha! That would stop you,
             wouldn't it!

WORKER   Oh...He wouldn't do anything like that. He's too
             polite.

SMOKER   You never know. After all, He does work in mysterious ways His wonders to perform. Nobody really knows what the rules are. Something that's polite to you or me might be very rude to Him. Look. Suppose you say, "Good morning, God, how are you?" That's pleasant enough, right?

WORKER   Sure.

SMOKER   Yeah, but He's the one who decides whether it's going to be a good morning or not. So your saying good morning could be taken as a very presumptuous command.

WORKER   Oh, now...

SMOKER   Not only that, but if you ask Him "How are you?" you're implying that He's changeable; that He isn't perfect. He could have you up for blasphemy just for saying hello.

                            Pause.

WORKER   Why are you being so negative?

SMOKER   Because I don't think anybody's thought this whole Tower business through properly. It might scare Him.

WORKER   Scare God? Come on.

SMOKER   Well then, maybe just make Him mad. What if we arrive and He says, "What the hell is the matter with you wise guys? Why can't you die like everybody else?"

WORKER   Well, if that happens, we'll just apologize and go back.

SMOKER   Yeah, but if Heaven is as great as everybody says, I think we'll find it very difficult to settle back down on the farm again.

WORKER	You never did like the farm. I think you just don't like work!
SMOKER	Not true! I like farming. I don't mind working at all, when I can see some point to it.
WORKER	Oh, you're just being a defeatist. You're afraid of the unknown. Anyway, look. If He really doesn't want us to get to Heaven by building this Tower, then He won't let us get to Heaven by building this Tower, that's all. He'll stop us.
SMOKER	How? How's He gonna stop us?
WORKER	Well, He could make the whole thing collapse and kill us all, if He wants to be a bastard about it.
SMOKER	Yeah, sure. He makes the whole thing collapse, and He kills us all, and we all die, and we all wind up in Heaven anyway. Precisely because we were building this thing. Nope.
WORKER	Well, He could stop us any way He wants to! He could make us all forget what we're doing; He could make our tools disappear. He could call up a thunderstorm, scare the crap out of us. He's the Almighty! He doesn't have to wait until we get up there and then send us back.
SMOKER	*(chuckling)* Come to think of it, waiting until we get up there and then sending us back would be a very just punishment.
WORKER	Oh, for Heaven's sake, don't give Him any bright ideas.
	A gloomy silence. The WORKER, *now thoroughly discouraged contemplates the distance they have come and the distance they have yet to go. The* SMOKER *smokes and thinks.*

SMOKER   Hey, whose bright idea was this, anyway? Who suggested we start building this Tower in the first place?

WORKER   I don't know...Some smartass a few generations back. Nobody remembers.

SMOKER   Because it occurs to me that if God didn't want us to build this thing, He would have stopped us a long time ago. He wouldn't even have given the original smartass the idea.

WORKER   *(thinking it through)* That's true...but He did...so He does. There! Ha! There, you see? Proof! From your own mouth! He obviously doesn't mind a bit.

SMOKER   Maybe not...I dunno...But if He did originally inspire us with the idea, then just maybe, He's planning something nasty.

WORKER   Oh, you just don't have any faith at all, do you? Why should He be planning something nasty? God made the world! He made you and me! He's on our side.

SMOKER   *(considering)* He did make the Garden of Eden...

WORKER   Right!

SMOKER   And Adam and Eve...

WORKER   Right again!

SMOKER   *(innocently)* And the Serpent...*(looking at the WORKER)*

WORKER   *(after a brief pause)* Well...yeah...okay... Hmm.

SMOKER   You see, I get the feeling that He has this thing for dramatic endings. He seems to like getting into the confrontation after the story has gone on a bit, rather than nipping it in the bud.

WORKER   Maybe He likes getting His name in the Bible.

SMOKER   Maybe. Maybe He just likes giving people lessons they won't forget.

WORKER   *(exasperated)* I see. So. According to you, the whole Tower is just doomed to failure, hm?

SMOKER   *(exasperated)* No, no, no, now I didn't say that. I just think He may find it offensive, that's all.

WORKER   He'll love it! Why, may I ask, do you assume that He's going to be offended? I would think He'd be flattered! I know that if a bunch of people went to this kind of trouble to get to me, I'd be tickled pink. Who knows? We don't know! Maybe when we arrive He'll come rushing over, hollering, "Glory be! You built that great huge Tower just to come up and visit? Just to visit little old Me? Well, glory be! Glory be to Me!" Maybe he'll have us over for dinner.

SMOKER   Yeah, but there are more traditional means of approach. Like meditation and prayers and good works.

WORKER   Yeah, so?

SMOKER   So since He's made these methods traditional, I would think He probably favours them.

WORKER   Aha! I see! So that's why you sit around on your ass cloudgazing while I'm trying to get the work done!

SMOKER   *(pleased with the rationale)* Yeah! Yeah, that's one way of looking at it.

WORKER   Right. Right. Just suppose He were to look down at the two of us here.

SMOKER   Okay.

WORKER	He looks at me, getting my hands nice and filthy with the grime of honest toil...
SMOKER	Oh, He'll love you. Haven't you heard the bit about cleanliness and Godliness?
WORKER	At least I'm working for His greater glory. What are you doing? Absolutely nothing, except to pollute His atmosphere with your foul tobacco. Who do you think He'll like best?
SMOKER	At least I'm quiet! At least I'm grateful for the world He's given me, and I trust Him to take me to the next world in His own sweet time. Not like you, banging and sawing, storming the Pearly Gates, trying to impress him with this— runaway technology. Who do you think He'll like best?
WORKER	*(after a brief pause)* I sing hymns to Him. I'm always singing hymns to Him.
SMOKER	I've noticed.
WORKER	You never sing hymns to Him.
SMOKER	Don't jump to conclusions. Maybe I sing them silently.
WORKER	Well, I sing mine nice and loud. I'm not ashamed of mine. I'll bet He really enjoys mine.
SMOKER	Does He?
WORKER	*(starting low and sweet and unctuously pious)* Holy, holy, holy, Lord God Almighty, Early in the morning Our song shall rise to Thee ...
SMOKER	*(louder, over the* WORKER's *hymn, beginning during the line "Early in the morning")*

SMOKER   The Lord's my shepherd,
I'll not want,
He makes me down to lie
In pastures green,
He leadeth me
The quiet waters by.

WORKER   *(raising the volume, and taking revenge by
starting on the* SMOKER*'s line "In pastures
green...")*

Mine eyes have seen the Glory of the coming of
the Lord,
He is trampling through the vintage where the
grapes of wrath are stor'd;
He hath loos'd the fearful lightning of His
terrible swift sword,
His truth is...

SMOKER   *(swinging, jiving, snapping his fingers, coming
in somewhere around "fearful lightning...")*

Swing low, sweet chariot,
Coming for to carry me home,
Swing low, sweet chariot,
Coming for to carry me...

WORKER   *(full volume, grand opera, all stops out; from
Handel's "Messiah")*

Hallelujah! Hallelujah!
Hallelujah, Hallelujah, Halle-e-lu-jaahh!
For the Lord God Omni-i-potent reigneth...

SMOKER   *(half singing along, half shouting)*

Hallelujah! Hallelujah!

BOTH   *(screaming at each other in fury)* Hallelujah!
Hallelujah! Hallelujah!

They are interrupted by a huge and angry thunderclap and a profound dimming and flickering of the lights. They stop and look up for a moment, and then dive for a hiding place (in the original production, the two actors had worked their way to the top of the step-ladder during the hymns then, down the ladder to cower on a small platform built across its lower strut).
They hide, quaking and gazing up at the storm rumbling and flickering for several moments before slowly dying out in a sulky muttering and rumbling. The lights steady at a dimmer level than the bright sunshine we had before. A pause.

SMOKER (*with awe and fear*) Maybe we should cut out the bullshit.

WORKER (*with awe and fear*) I don't think He's too pleased with either one of us at the moment.

SMOKER He probably feels we're presuming

WORKER (*frustrated*) Yes, but presuming to what? Presuming to find favour with the Almighty? What's wrong with that?

SMOKER Well, maybe we shouldn't be putting each other down in order to do it.

WORKER (*with some self pity*) Perhaps...I wish He'd tell us what the hell He wants from us. I mean, I'm doing my best.

SMOKER I know; it's very trying.

WORKER Trying is the word for it.

SMOKER Hey, maybe He just wants us to cooperate. Get along. Work together.

WORKER	Work together? Huh. I know what that means. That's where I came in. With me working and you goofing off.
SMOKER	No, no, I don't mean just on the Tower. I mean on anything. He may not want us to work on the Tower at all. But if we're going to work on something, maybe He figures we shouldn't fight over it.
WORKER	Okay. Well. What is there to work on?
SMOKER	I dunno.
WORKER	Look. As I pointed out a short time ago, you might as well work on the Tower as on anything else. Helps pass the time.
SMOKER	Hm.
WORKER	*(his idea gaining momentum)* And...judging from that little thunder routine, He is perfectly capable of expressing His displeasure when He wants to. Ergo, He hasn't previously wanted to...ergo, the Tower is an acceptable project on which to work.
SMOKER	*(considers this for a moment)* Maybe He didn't know we were around until just now.
WORKER	What?
SMOKER	We were singing pretty loudly. Maybe our singing attracted His attention. Maybe He hadn't noticed us before.
WORKER	How could He not have noticed us before? He sees the little sparrow fall...We're building the tallest goddamn Tower in human history! I'm hammering nails at top volume. You're letting cigarette smoke drift up into the stratosphere. How could He not have noticed us?
SMOKER	Maybe He was asleep.

Pause.

WORKER   *(horrified)* Do you think maybe we woke him up?

SMOKER   It's a possibility.

WORKER   That's not a very nice thing to do, is it?

SMOKER   Well, if I were the Almighty, trying to get some sleep, and two guys were building a tower and singing hymns one floor below me, I imagine I might get mildly pissed off.

WORKER   *(after a pause)* Maybe we should apologize.

SMOKER   Maybe we should.

> *They kneel side by side in attitudes of prayer. They pray, ad lib, almost silently, in very low whispers, but we can see their mouths moving, and they tend to gesture. Their approach vacillates between abject flattery and high-pressure persuasion.*

SMOKER   *(finishing first)* Amen...

> *The* WORKER *goes on, ad lib; we can barely hear him, but it sounds like he is blaming the noise on the* SMOKER.

SMOKER   Amen!

WORKER   Amen.

> *Pause. They look around.*

WORKER   Any reply?

SMOKER   No. You?

WORKER   No...He never says nothin' to me anyway.

*The lights have been brightening back
to sunlight.*

SMOKER   Well, maybe we calmed Him down a little. The
sun's shining...everything seems all right!

WORKER   *(with apparent heartiness, but underneath, a new
unease)* Yeah! Everything...seems the same...

SMOKER   *(after a brief pause).*Well! I'm gonna have another
cigarette.

WORKER   Right! You do that. I'm gonna...get back to
work...Shalom.

SMOKER   Shazam. *(the WORKER does not move)*
Something wrong?

WORKER   You know there's something wrong.

SMOKER   Yeah...Hey, do you get the feeling we're being
watched?

*As soon as the thought is voiced, they
look frantically around them, high and
low, upstage and into the audience, and
wind up looking back at each other.*

WORKER   Nobody around.

SMOKER   Nope.

WORKER   Just...you and me! Heh, heh.

SMOKER   Yup.

WORKER   We are definitely being watched.

SMOKER   *(equally nervous, but a bit more in control)* Yes.
Definitely. There's somebody behind us.

WORKER   *(starting to panic)* How can there be somebody
behind us? We're facing each other!

SMOKER　　　　Yeah! I know...

　　　　　　　　Pause, as they both realize the identity
　　　　　　　　of the watcher.

WORKER　　　　Look busy. *(handing the* SMOKER *a tool)* Here.
　　　　　　　　Get to work.

SMOKER　　　　Right.

　　　　　　　　They both start to work, whistling
　　　　　　　　ostentatiously. They work for a few
　　　　　　　　moments, still paranoid then a couple of
　　　　　　　　touches of thunder sound

SMOKER　　　　Hey, will ya pass the gerzil?

WORKER　　　　*(preoccupied)* What?

SMOKER　　　　Kindly pass the gerzil.

　　　　　　　　Pause.

WORKER　　　　What the fump is a gerzil?

　　　　　　　　Pause.

SMOKER　　　　The gerzil, you plink! It's in the gool fronk.

　　　　　　　　Pause. All work has stopped.

WORKER　　　　Are...you playing some kind of a shnobbly frape
　　　　　　　　with me? What is this crimple?

　　　　　　　　Pause.

SMOKER　　　　What the fnerch are you scroggling about?

WORKER　　　　All right, come on, nerkle. Flumb it.

SMOKER　　　　Aw, cub it ouch!

	Pause, as the WORKER *seethes for a moment; then he loses his temper.*
WORKER	I have had enunch! You blaw gap futhermudding summon afitch!
SMOKER	Why you cog spugging hansard! Don't you spall me grames!
WORKER	Plimp!
SMOKER	Grutch!
WORKER	*(grabbing the* SMOKER *by his collar)* Chiltz!
SMOKER	*(doing likewise)* Patser! *(as the lights dim and a blast of thunder sounds,* SMOKER, *realizing, points to the sky)* See? See? It's Rib! It's Gob! He's blogging argle! Befuzz we're gilding the Townsend! He's mailing us gawk funny!
WORKER	I stan't undercand a ilerd you snay! You're glonking funny!
SMOKER	*(overlapping slightly)* I stan't undercand a flerd you snay! You're glonking funny!
	Thunder up. They look at the sky. The SMOKER *suddenly starts pulling out planks, and throwing them down. Thunder under.*
WORKER	You can't doobers! We're too curst to Heaven! You don't understand!
SMOKER	You can't doobers! We're too toast eleven! You don't stand under! You're not talking the same language any more!
WORKER	Borg?
SMOKER	*(gesticulating)* You're...not...talking...the same...language...anymore!

WORKER   Glop?

SMOKER   You're not...ohh...

> *More thunder. The* SMOKER *pulls down a plank. The thunder abruptly stops and the lights brighten. The* WORKER *grabs the plank putting it back up: the thunder starts again and the lights dim. The* SMOKER *pulls it down: thunder stops, lights brighten. The* WORKER, *experimenting, puts it up: thunder starts, lights dim. The* WORKER, *his eye on the sky, slowly hands the plank to the* SMOKER: *thunder fades, sky fades up. The* SMOKER *continues dismantling in silence, while the* WORKER *looks on, bewildered. The sun is now bright, the sky peaceful. The* SMOKER *glances up, sees the* WORKER *feeling useless and silently offers him the cigarette he refused at the beginning of the play. Slowly the* WORKER *lights up and sits back, still trying to figure this thing out. The* SMOKER *works, the* WORKER *smokes. Gradually the* WORKER's *frown fades, and he is just beginning to relax and enjoy watching the birds when the lights slowly fade out.*

> *The End.*

HEDGES

DAVE CARLEY

Born and raised in Peterborough, Ontario, Dave Carley explored careers in law and journalism before realizing his true calling was writing for theatre. His 1988 play *Midnight Madness* has been produced across Canada and was published by Summerhill Press. *Writing With Our Feet* premiered in 1990 and has been produced in a number of Canadian and American cities, and has been published by Blizzard Press. *Hedges* is Carley's only play for teenagers and, since its premiere in 1985 at the Merrickville Century Theatre, it has been produced across Canada, the United States, and in Japan. Dave Carley lives in Toronto, where he is script editor on CBC Radio's Stereodrama.

THE CHARACTERS

The cast of *Hedges* can number four or six, though the latter is preferable. If the smaller cast is necessary, the roles of DON and DEBBIE JONES, and PETER and JUDY SMITH, can be played by one actor each. Slight alterations to the script would be necessary.

THE SET

The set should be simple.

THE TIME

The time is now.

Hedges was first produced August, 1985 in Smith's Falls, Ontario by the Smith's Falls and District Youth Committee, under the auspices of International Youth Year 1985, and in conjunction with the Merrickville Century Theatre with the following cast:

HEDGE	*Helen Bretzke*
WIDGET	*Kate Egan*
PETER SMITH	*William Hurman*
JUDY SMITH	*Felica Kelso*
DEBBIE JONES	*Karen D'Alessio*
DON JONES	*Christopher McLeod*

Directed by Arnold Connerty.
Assistant to the director: Charis Kelso.

Hedges was a winner of the 1985 Creative Peacemaking Award. The play has been produced across Canada, in the United States and, in 1990, was the headline production at the Kanagawa International Arts Festival in Japan.

A number of people have given valuable assistance in the development of this script, and special thanks go to Marion Gilsenan, Glenda MacFarlane, the Kelso family of Smith's Falls, Arnold Connerty, Bea Quarrie, and the many dedicated peace activists in Peterborough, Ontario.
This play is dedicated to Greg and Laura, Georgia and Robert, and Liam.

AUTHOR'S INTRODUCTION

Back in 1985 Marion Gilsenan asked me if I would write a play to commemorate International Youth Year. Ms Gilsenan, was running a small theatre in the eastern Ontario village of Merrickville and she needed something that was performable by students-on-grants. I quickly accepted her commission, despite the fact I found the prospect of writing a play for teenagers intimidating. I thought I'd have to start hanging around schoolyards, learning a radical new vocabulary, and I didn't have the foggiest notion what the then-pressing teenage concerns might be.

It took me a few months to realize that actually the worst thing I could do was to write in a "different" language. Nor could I write about something that wasn't of vital concern to my own post-teen self. The only subjects I could really speak about with any authority and credibility were the ones that troubled my own heart and, if those concerns were truly important, my student performers and audiences would find a way of relating to them.

I've always been involved in the human rights and peace movements so they seemed like logical starting points. The arms race was in high gear in 1985 and there was no clear Canadian foreign policy. (Could we expect anything different from our wannabe congressman-Prime Minister, Brian Mulroney?) Officially, we were toeing an aggressive American line: Star Wars, Cruise Missiles, arming Europe -- it was hardware, hardware, hardware. Privately, however, most Canadians were expressing unease at what seemed to be a mad, genocidal arms race. The mood of dissent was good, except that it often smacked of smugness, with an implicit assumption that all evil generated from south of the border and if Canada ever got a Prime Minister who was capable of independent, sober second thought, well heck, we'd be a big force for peace in our time.

Smug is the one thing Canadians have no right to be. When I wrote *Hedges* Canada was an active participant in the arms trade -- in 1985 selling more than $1.75 billion in arms to various governments around the world. (The figures only pertained to finished products, and didn't include raw materials that might be converted at some later date by the destination country. Those figures also assumed that all sales are being recorded, and revealed.) We were selling everything from boots to sophisticated missile guidance systems, both to the Americans and to such human rights pariahs as Iraq, Indonesia, Uganda and China. Hardly the actions of a noble, peace-loving people! So when Canadians blithely went about denouncing the militaristic Yanks, I thought they should know what was going on just down their own street. I had a lot of anger in my heart -- anger and shame. It made *Hedges* easy to write.

I tried to make *Hedges* a physical piece, so that the energy of student performers (my intended actors) could be unleashed. I added humour, not to sugar-coat my message about our complicity in the arms race, but to hopefully give the rather dark ending even more bite. The play doesn't need an elaborate set and actually works better with less clutter. A few cutouts of houses to suggest a bucolic, typical Canadian suburb are sufficient.

Hedges premiered in 1985 and, since then, has had about twenty other productions. It even got on to a kind of Methodist youth network in the States, and the directors there have told me that the play makes just as much sense to American teenagers -- that when I talk about Canada's involvement, they extrapolate that to mean their own community's weaponsmongering. In 1990 *Hedges* was featured at the Kanagawa International Arts Festival in Japan, where I'm told it received wild acclaim.

This is not to say anything more about the play than to suggest it remains as unfortunately relevant in this "post-cold war" era as it did in 1985. Despite some bleatings by sometime External Affairs Minister Joe Clark about legislating an end to the international arms trade, our government continues to promote arms exports. There is still blood on our hands -- $1.25 billion of it in 1989, for example.

Students and teachers wishing to receive up-to-date information on Canadian arms dealings should contact their local peace group. My source, and a great resource for us all, is Project Ploughshares, Conrad Grebel College, Waterloo, Ontario N2L 3G6. Phone: (519) 888-6541. Teachers can also get resource materials, including Ruth Leger Savard's *Canadian Teachers' Guide to Accompany World Military and Social Expenditures* from the Pembina Institute, Box 7558, Drayton Valley, Alberta TOE 0M0. Phone: (403) 542-6272. Fax: (403) 542-6464.

Dave Carley

HEDGES

The play begins with HEDGE *alone on stage, standing on the well-marked line between the* SMITH *and* JONES *properties.* HEDGE *will travel up and down this line -- but not off it.*

HEDGE   I know what you're thinking: I'm just an ordinary, run-of-the-mill hedge. I can live with that. I was born cedar and sure, I know how most of you feel about that, too. You think cedars are ugly. We're a dime a dozen. You prefer lilacs. *(shrugging)* Your loss. I smell good and I stay green all year. Small people use me for shade. I'm thick enough for hiding stuff -- oh yeah, I've got my secrets; all hedges do. But hey, I mind my own business. I don't ask questions. You start asking too many questions, you get chopped down. On the other hand, if you don't ask enough questions, you get chopped down, too. Jeez. *(pause)* I don't smoke, don't drink or swear; I don't even cheat on my income tax. I'm a model citizen. OK, OK -- I've got a few mosquitoes, but that's it. Maybe some caterpillars and the odd mouse. Riff raff. Nothing dangerous. *(beat)* I sure never deserved what I got from you guys.

There might be offstage music here, or choral advertising: "Widgetworld!".

HEDGE   Humans. You make me sick.

WIDGET enters, gladhanding, with false bonhommie. He's a master salesman.

WIDGET   Hiya pal. Lookin' good. *(to audience with sudden, overwhelming "sincerity". Study: Brian Mulroney)* If there was any way I could turn back the hands of time and undo the awful events of the past few months *(shaking head in sorrow)* Oh gosh...Oh gee...

HEDGE   The whole thing was your fault!

WIDGET   Hedge, my friend, please! I had nothing to do with it. Nil, zilcho!

HEDGE   You had everything to do with it. You were the catalyst. You were the accelerator and you should've been the brakes.

WIDGET   A nice turn of phrase, but you don't have a firm grip on logic. My only interest was for the well-being of the parties involved.

HEDGE   Why don't we let the general public be the judge of that. *(indicating audience)* That's a quality jury out there. Let's fly it by them and see what they think.

WIDGET   *(pause)* Why don't we. No sweat off my back. I've got nothing to hide. My hands are clean...

　　　　　　　　　　HEDGE *clears throat as if to disagree.* WIDGET *moves in front of him, and gets speechy, going on the offensive.*

WIDGET   My friends. Hedge here, this motley, blight-ridden haven for leaf-chewing caterpillars and dirty birds, this collector of blowing newspapers, catcher of flying plastic debris, this low-rent hotel for refuse...

　　　　　　　　　　HEDGE *has been self-consciously discarding bits of garbage as* WIDGET *speaks.*

WIDGET   Hedge seems to think his current physical failure is my fault.

HEDGE   I can prove it.

WIDGET

He's feeling a little on the hard done-by side of life because things haven't worked out for him. He is, after all, just another cedar hedge. I mean, he gets a bit messed up and he feels this great need to cast blame all over the place.

HEDGE

Not all over the place! Just at you!

WIDGET

Ah well, today I'm the villain. *(indicating audience)* Just watch, tomorrow he'll be blaming you, too.

HEDGE

I won't!

WIDGET

Why not? They're Canadians, just like you and me. If you're going to dump all over me then you have to dump on them, too.

HEDGE

You're grandstanding. You're trying to get them on your side. Just get on with the story and save the fancy arguments for later.

> *There can be inspiring "Widgetworld" music welling up under* WIDGET's *next speech.*

WIDGET

My name is Widget and I'm the fourth generation Widget to be in the hardware business in this town. That's quite a record eh? In this entire country I doubt there's one house or barn that doesn't contain at least one Widget whatchamacallit --

HEDGE

Weally.

WIDGET

Because we sell everything. Cheap. Sure, we make a little money here and there. *(sharply)* There's no law against that. Widgets are community pillars. We employ lots of people. We give money to charities.

HEDGE

This is sounding a lot like an ad.

WIDGET   It's a public service announcement. Did I say we employ lots of people? And we tie up all our garbage in almost-biodegradable plastic bags. We're part of this community and we make it a better place to live. And it's an awfully, awfully nice town.

HEDGE   It was.

WIDGET   Yes, it's an awfully nice town chockfull of awfully nice people. Which made it all the more surprising and -- yes -- hurtful when open warfare broke out between the Smiths and the Joneses. Personally, and this is speaking as a respectable merchant, I was horrified. Dismayed. Depressed.

HEDGE   Personally, and this is speaking as a hedge, I was wrecked!

WIDGET   We were all shaken up.

HEDGE   Shaken up! Look at me! *(pointing at* WIDGET*)* And it's all because of you --

WIDGET   *(cutting in, over the last sentence)* But for this craven collection of curling leaves to insinuate that I , Widget -- Mr. Honest -- Mr. Nice, to even hint that I could have had anything to do with it... it's outrageous! It's so outrageous it makes me laugh! *(silly laugh)* See -- I'm laughing. *(silly laugh again)*

HEDGE   But it *was* your fault.

WIDGET   IT WAS NOT! *(remembering to do silly laugh)* The very idea is laughable. *(laughing)*

HEDGE   Are you going to tell this story, or will I?

WIDGET   No one'd believe a hedge. *(gathering composure)* This is primarily the tale of two families, the Smiths and the Joneses.

WIDGET   *(continued)* Those are not their real names, of course. The Smiths and the Joneses: two ordinary families separated by one exceedingly ordinary hedge. Don and Debbie Jones, and Fifi --

HEDGE   *(disgusted)* Fifi.

WIDGET   They lived at Number 3, Silverfish Crescent. Peter and Judy Smith lived next door, at Number 5.

HEDGE   Plus Rex.

WIDGET   Rex isn't in the story yet. *(brightly)* But, oh gosh -- here's Peter now!

> PETER SMITH *enters, smiling and waving like a game show contestant.*

WIDGET   Yes, Peter is a law-abiding nice man, a teacher at the local high school -- a guidance counsellor?

PETER   That's right Widget. I tell students where to go.

WIDGET   I'll bet you do. Anyway, welcome to our little parable.

> PETER *walks to his area, by* HEDGE. *He might make a fond gesture in* HEDGE's *direction, which will be rebuffed.*

WIDGET   As you can see, Peter Smith isn't the handsomest man in the world --

HEDGE   Or the smartest --

WIDGET   But there was something about him that Judy Smith found attractive, so she married him.

> JUDY SMITH *enters, smiling and waving.*

WIDGET	It's Judy! The office manager at a local insurance agency, Judy Smith enjoys golf, embroidery and gardening.
JUDY	Especially gardening, Widget. My petunias are the pride of the suburb. Hiya Hedge.
WIDGET	Last year Peter and Judy Smith spent over a thousand dollars in my store. Items for the new rec room Peter's building. Gardening supplies for Judy...You'll never hear me say a bad word about the Smiths, ever.
HEDGE	Hmmpff.

> DEBBIE JONES *enters, then* DON *shyly.*

WIDGET	Don and Debbie Jones are equally nice folks. Debbie works at the bank, in a position of trust and responsibility.
DEBBIE	Although I wasn't born here, I've come to love this town.
WIDGET	Aw, that's nice. That's swell. *(to* HEDGE*)* Isn't that nice? *(to* DEBBIE*)* And you're a fan of opera, I hear.
DEBBIE	*(trilling and laughing)* That's right. *(trilling)*
HEDGE	Oh Lordy.
WIDGET	Where's your husband. Oh Don -- there you are. Don, step forward a sec willya? Don't be shy. You're among friends. Don here owns the variety store on Water Street. How's it going, anyway?
DON	Good. *(pause)*
WIDGET	Uh, would you care to elaborate?
DON	Up?

WIDGET   Ah...up.

DON   Up lots.

WIDGET   Great.

DON   Lots and lots.

WIDGET   Great pal. *(continuing with story)* Last year --

DON   Really really up!

WIDGET   Really up.

DON   Really up lots.

WIDGET   I'm glad.

DON   Lots really up.

WIDGET   *(pushing* DON *back a bit, trying to continue)* Last year --

DON   A whole pile really lots up.

WIDGET   Shut up!

DON   Thank you!

WIDGET   Last year Don and Debbie Jones spent nearly two thousand dollars in my store. They are fine, upstanding citizens and you'll never hear me say a word against them.

HEDGE   Fifi.

WIDGET   How could I forget! The Jones have a small schnauzer -- they're the ones that look like dustballs on legs. Fifi. Come on out Fifi and take a bow.

          All six look in the direction of the JONES' *house.*

WIDGET   Come on Fifi!

>*They still look.* DON *whistles.*

DEBBIE   Come out wittle wamb chop.

>HEDGE *groans. An invisible* FIFI *enters, and all six mime watching her progress. The following endearments and disparagements overlap.*

DEBBIE   Here she comes --

DON   Sweetie pie hi fi --

DEBBIE   Lambie chop chop --

DON   Daddy's baby --

HEDGE   Honestly --

DON   Twittie twittie wing ding --

DEBBIE   Doggie honey bunny wunny --

WIDGET   It *is* pretty sickening.

HEDGE   You have to wonder.

DON   Daddy's wittle tiger.

DEBBIE   Tweetie sweetie --

DON   Diggity doggie --

>FIFI *has run by* DEBBIE *and* DON *and around the others. They all follow with their eyes until* FIFI *comes to the* SMITH *side of* HEDGE. *At this point the* JONESES *suddenly find something else to do.*

DEBBIE	*(nervous laugh)* Oh ha, Don, look at that uh bird up there --
DON	Oh yeah, it's a bird...*(improvising)*
HEDGE	*(meanwhile; trying to kick* FIFI *away)* Get lost. Get lost you mutt. Scram fleabag. Get lost. *(then, as* FIFI *unloads)* Aw come on...Fifi...
PETER	Well!
JUDY	That damn dog!
PETER	Where's my shovel!
WIDGET	No wait -- we haven't reached that part of the story yet.
PETER	But Fifi's --
WIDGET	We'll get to Fifi in a second. I want to tell them about the pride you took in Hedge.
PETER	Oh. Okay.
WIDGET	Because you were proud of him.
PETER	We groomed him like a golf green.
DEBBIE	*(snipping)* You like that, don't you.
HEDGE	Oo - oo, yes. Uh huh.
JUDY	Would you like your sides done?
HEDGE	Yeah, do it to me, Judy, baby.
WIDGET	They took wonderful care of Hedge. I sold them only the finest organic fertilizer and sprays, and they used the gentlest of clippers. I sharpened them every month...

HEDGE	*(under, in ecstasy)* More, more. Uh huh, oh yeah...
JUDY	*(proudly)* There were birds in our hedge.
DON	And the wonderful scent of cedar.
DEBBIE	And healthful bugs.
HEDGE	The kind of bugs you'd take home to mother, if you were a hedge.
PETER	Good urban insects, susceptible to sprays --
DEBBIE	And nice birds, eating the nice sprayed bugs...
WIDGET	The funny thing about Hedge was that no one was quite sure how he got here in the first place.
PETER	We moved here six years ago and he was already *(indicating)* that tall.
DEBBIE	And we've been here eight -- he was here then.
HEDGE	*(possibly over noble music)* I always believed I came from the forest. From the wilds of the Canadian Shield. From the land of the wolf and the bear, where hedges are hedges and cedars stand tall and tough and proud. My mother was probably a hundred feet tall! I betcha she had bugs on her like you wouldn't believe! And my Dad, maybe he was a Douglas Fir and --
WIDGET	They say that good hedges make good neighbours, and, in the early days, the Smiths and the Joneses got along famously.
JUDY	*(sees DEBBIE dialling phone)* Oh, she's calling us. *(picking up phone)* Hello?
DEBBIE	Judy, it's Debbie. Don and I were wondering if you and Peter would like to come over tonight.

JUDY   How lovely. *(to* PETER*)* They're asking us over!

PETER   *(happily)* Super!

DEBBIE   It's time we progressed to the next stage.

JUDY   Oh gosh, how exciting! We'll be right there!

HEDGE   They were taking a correspondence course in dancing. You know, one of those things where you send away and for just a few dollars every week you get a tape in the mail with instructions --

JUDY   Which one are we at now?

DON   Well, we've done the Charleston and the jitterbug.

PETER   And the twist and the gavotte --

DEBBIE   I wouldn't mind square dancing again.

DON   I kind of thought it was time for --

JUDY & DEBBIE   *(holding up tape and reading)* Tang-oh!

> *Tango music up and awkward but fun attempts at doing it, with spouses switched.*

WIDGET   Yes, they were ultracompatible neighbours all right. Life on Silverfish Crescent couldn't've been happier. It's hard to say what broke it all up.

> *Dancing and music stops dead.*

PETER   Some said it was Fifi.

DON   Never.

DEBBIE	Not Fifi Weefy.
HEDGE	I'm with Smith on this. Fifi started it.
WIDGET	The simple fact was, the Smith side of Hedge seemed to give Fifi all the privacy her schnauzer sensibilities required - and this didn't sit well with the Smiths.
PETER	*(handing over money)* Shovel!
WIDGET	Aluminum, plastic, snow, shiny --
PETER	A little one. Fifi-sized.
WIDGET	Ah, I understand. *(handing over shovel)* The Smiths made a real point of lobbing Fifi's autographs back over the hedge into the Jones' yard.
HEDGE	*(ducking)* Careful!
WIDGET	But Don and Debbie Jones continued to let Fifi roam wherever she wanted, so the Smiths upped the stakes.
JUDY	*(approaching WIDGET, waving money)* I need a dog collar and a chain. A *big* collar and a *thick* chain. For Rex.
HEDGE	The Smiths' new dog was incredibly large.
WIDGE	Huge.
HEDGE	Little Fifi Weefy took one look at Rex and decided to stay on her side of me.
WIDGET	Rex, on the other hand, found himself irresistably drawn to the Jones' side --
HEDGE	Where he dug holes.
WIDGET	Some vague genetic impulse --

DON	He's at it again!
DEBBIE	My poor flat lawn!
HEDGE	Rex had it looking like an open pit mine!
WIDGET	Don was in the store a couple of days later, buying defense materials.

> WIDGET *hands* DON *a large shovel in exchange for money.*

DON	And while you're at it, give me some lime.
HEDGE	Lime!
DON	I heard somewhere dogs won't walk on lime. I'm going to lime a five-foot swath around that hedge.
HEDGE	Lime's not in my contract!
DEBBIE	Hold still!
DON	It's for your own good. Quit twitching.
HEDGE	It stings!
DEBBIE	It'll also keep Rex out.
HEDGE	Really? Just a bit, then.
WIDGET	Because of the dogs, and the lime, the atmosphere -- and some of the lawn on Silverfish Crescent -- got a bit poisoned.
HEDGE	Unkind words were exchanged.
DON	Insect.
JUDY	Larva.
DEBBIE	Pupae.

PETER	Bug.
HEDGE	That night Don and Debbie tangoed alone. So did the Smiths.

> *Music. The couples are tangoing, but separately. It obviously isn't as much fun.*

DON	Tango!
JUDY	Tango!
DEBBIE	There's something missing.
PETER	This doesn't feel right.
HEDGE	But they wouldn't admit, even to themselves, that it's a lot more fun to tango with your neighbour's spouse, than with your own...
JUDY	*(false happiness, so* DON *and* DEBBIE *will hear)* Tangohhh! Wahoooo!
DEBBIE	*(so* PETER *and* JUDY *will hear)* Tangohhh! Hot hot hot!
DON	I bet they're not having --
DEBBIE	as much fun as we are, and --
PETER	I bet they wish they could --
JUDY	be over here with us and --
PETER	I wish we could be --
DEBBIE	over there with them.
JUDY	If they want to tango with us --
DON	they can darn well apologize --

ALL   First!

                       *There's a pause. The neighbours all look
                       expectantly at each other.* WIDGET
                       springs into action.

WIDGET   Sale on lime! Lime -- half price! Shovels! *(to
                       DEBBIE)* There must be something I can sell
                       you...

                       DON *and* DEBBIE *confer.*

DEBBIE   As a matter of fact, I'd like a garbage lid.

WIDGET   Certainly.

DEBBIE   And I'll need a hockey helmet. Do you have any
                       horns?

                       WIDGET *feels his head.*

DEBBIE   I mean, for sale. *(pointing to two gas funnels)*
                       Those'll do.

                       Money changes hands, and DEBBIE
                       exits.

HEDGE   The thing was, Debbie Jones was a frustrated
                       opera singer. When she was a kid, everyone said
                       it'd only be a few years before she was singing
                       all over the world. People in the know said
                       there'd be two names on everyone's lips: *(naming
                       a popular female rock star)* and Debbie.

WIDGET   But it never happened. Debbie developed a
                       wobble in her warble and the jobs widdled away.
                       She never became a star --

HEDGE   But at night she'd practice. It was agony.

                       DEBBIE *re-enters in "Brunhilde" get-up,
                       with the funnels as horns and the
                       garbage can lid as her shield etc.*

DON   Yes dear, you may as well share the wealth. A talent like yours should be heard all over the world -- or at least over the hedge. *(laughing maliciously)*

DEBBIE   *(looking over* HEDGE*)* My public! How I adore my public!

                      DEBBIE *lets fly with a tentative trill. A branch or two falls off* HEDGE.

HEDGE   *(under, as trilling continues)* Oh no. Anything but this. I can't stand opera.

HEDGE   *(continued)* It's not natural for a hedge to listen to opera. *(more branches fall)* This is torture! Lime me, lime me! Bring back the dogs! Anything but this!

WIDGET   *(amused)* Which was exactly how the Smiths felt too!

PETER   They've gone too far!

JUDY   She's singing too high!

PETER   And too flat!

HEDGE   And too sharp! Do something! I beg you, do something!

DON   *(peering over at the* SMITHS*)* Keep it up, dear. They're hurting!

JUDY   *(starting to swoon)* Oh - oh - please - Peter, let's move...

PETER   Hang in there honey. Bear up. *(to* WIDGET*)* I want a blaster. The biggest you've got. *(waving money, getting radio)* And tapes. Who's the most obnoxious, talentless singer today?

WIDGET   *(naming a singer)*

PETER   Sounds good to me! *(handing over money, taking tape)* This is war. *(inserting tape)* Crank up the volume and a one and a two -- FIRE!

> *The noise should be mimed.* HEDGE *and* DON *and* DEBBIE *are blown back by a wall of sound. Everyone is shouting soundlessly, and clutching their ears. Leaves and branches fly off* HEDGE. FIFI *is blown offstage They begin miming "Turn it off" and* HEDGE *will slay the blaster with a branch.*

HEDGE   STOP! Ceasefire! This noise is killing me! We've got to talk, guys. Put that blaster away. Kill the opera, sister!

WIDGET   This is a free country, Hedge. If they want to play music...*(aside, sotto)* More batteries?

HEDGE   *(over) You* can afford to say that. *You're* making money from this and *you* live on the other side of town but they're driving me nuts! Look: when was the last time you saw a bird in these leaves? Or a half-decent bug? They all got wise and flew off but I'm stuck here and I want some peace and quiet. So can we talk?

> *The* SMITHS *and* JONESES *sit down on either side of* HEDGE. *To* WIDGET's *apparent worry, they seem to be starting a peace parley.*

HEDGE   That's nice. Everyone's settling down peacefully. Do this for me, eh guys? We'll have a little peace conference and live happily ever after...Debbie: you go first.

> *Throughout the following peace talk* WIDGET *will insert sotto voce phrases, promoting his lime and batteries and loud tapes etc., in an attempt to derail the conference.*

DEBBIE I'll tie up Fifi if you'll chain Rex.

> WIDGET *whispers in* PETER's *ear.*

PETER That's all very well, but Fifi is only one-tenth the size of Rex. If you really want to be fair, you'd have to tie up ten Fifis. And you'll have to include an unbreakable promise to never, ever sing opera anywhere in this universe, ever again. I've never heard anything so awful!

> DEBBIE *makes a noise of outrage and* WIDGET *has been whispering in* DON's *ear.*

DON That's a completely different issue -- we aren't discussing my wife's singing today. Besides, how can we be sure you won't let Rex out at night?

WIDGET Good point.

HEDGE I'll monitor them.

WIDGET Let them solve this themselves. They're adults. *(to* DON*)* So how 'bout another garbage lid? I'll give you a deal --

DON How much?

PETER *(to* JUDY*)* We should see about buying some more batteries --

HEDGE *(over)* And just like that, negotiations broke down. It was so maddening!

WIDGET So very upsetting! *(musing)* I wonder if I've got any bags of lime left --

HEDGE Some might say you had a vested interest in continuing this conflict.

WIDGET	I resent that! I'm a signatory of the Hardware Merchants Good Behaviour Treaty. *(reciting)* "I will never knowingly sell something to someone that can be used in an offensive manner." And I haven't. Everything I've sold was for defensive purposes only.
PETER	I need some glue.
WIDGET	Glue? Coming up! *(tangoing off, happily)* Glue glue glue! *(returning with pail of glue)* Glue glue glue...

> JUDY *is shaping the* JONES' *side of* HEDGE, *to make* HEDGE *making a rude gesture - finger up or thumb down.*

JUDY	Make it stick, honey!

> PETER *slaps on glue.* HEDGE's *arm locks into position.* DON *and* DEBBIE *see, and react.*

DON	Cut that out!
DEBBIE	The nerve!
HEDGE	Did I say it was "maddening"? I could give you a lot of other words: depressing, avoidable, painful. I'd been so green and so fragrant for so many years and now I was being destroyed by something so damn childish, so senseless, by an argument that no one could remember the reason for, by a fire they all knew how to start but none of them could put out...
DEBBIE	*(under last part of preceding, as she hands* WIDGET *a cheque)* Give me a chainsaw!

> DEBBIE *throws the chainsaw to* DON, *who immediately cuts off the branch.*

DON	Timber!

JUDY

(to WIDGET*)* Spraypaint!

> JUDY *hands* WIDGET *a stack of money and is handed a can of spraypaint which she tosses to* PETER.

PETER

(reading as he sprays) DON AND DEBBIE JONES ARE VERMIN!

> DON *grabs can from* PETER, *runs to* SMITH *side of* HEDGE, *and sprays:*

DEBBIE

(reading) KILL THE SMITHS!

> *The couples freeze in horror.* WIDGET *is nearby, at the ready.*

HEDGE

That stopped them for a few minutes. They glared at each other, spray cans clutched in their angry little hands, with only me separating them -- what was left of me, anyway -- and then they got right back to it. They had to finish what they started.

WIDGET

(handing over a can of kerosene to DON *and one to* PETER*)* If I'd ever guessed what the kerosene was for --

> DON *and* PETER *are dousing* HEDGE.

WIDGET

Or the matches, for that matter...

> DON, DEBBIE, PETER *and* JUDY *light matches.*

HEDGE

It's irrelevant who did it...who lit the match. I decided to pack it in. *(to* WIDGET, *sorrowfully)* If only you'd sit back and think about your role in all this -- if only you'd do that, I wouldn't feel that this was so meaningless...

> HEDGE *turns. The back of his T-shirt is blue. When the others eventually turn to join him the combined image of their shirts will be that of the globe; they form a globe, with their bodies linked together.*

WIDGET   Hedge? Hedge!

> *At his last appeal to* HEDGE, WIDGET *pulls his hands from his pockets, or in some other way provokes a little cloudfall of money. They fall to his feet and he contemplates them, then picks them up and begins stuffing them back in his pockets. He ignores* DON, DEBBIE, PETER *and* JUDY *and speaks directly to the audience.*

WIDGET   My friends! I'm as upset by all this as everyone else! I love hedges and sure -- that one was pretty obnoxious -- but even he didn't deserve what he got. I know that. But it isn't fair to pin it on me. I didn't know they'd behave that way!

> DON *and* DEBBIE *are turning. They have portions of the globe on their T-shirts, and they'll link up with* HEDGE.

Not Don and Debbie Jones. They're model citizens -- like you and me! Don had his store and Debbie loved the opera...

> PETER *and* JUDY *are turning, and join the forming globe.*

And Peter and Judy Smith -- they were good folk too! Nothing shabby about them! I can't imagine what got into them.

> *A bill or two flutters down.*

WIDGET   Seems crazy they got fighting like that.
                             (counting a bit of money) I know what you're
                             thinking. But you saw it all. I only sold them
                             the things they asked for; I didn't know what
                             they'd be using it all for. Remember: it's not the
                             gun that does the killing -- it's the person pulling
                             the trigger. *(counting the money again)* What
                             would you have done differently? What are you
                             doing differently? Sure -- you're the jury and you
                             can convict me of anything you want, but you
                             better be fair. Put yourself in my shoes...

                                       WIDGET *has pulled a Canadian flag
                                       from his pocket. He might be wiping
                                       his brow with it. It should not be
                                       completely unfurled, but it should be
                                       very clear what it is.*

WIDGET   Or are you already in them?

                                       *The others turn back and look at the
                                       audience.* WIDGET *looks up and out at
                                       the audience too.*

                                       Black.

                                       The End.

HEROES

KEN MITCHELL

Novelist, poet, actor, and teacher, Ken Mitchell was born in 1940 in Moose Jaw, and educated at the University of Saskatchewan. He has written plays for radio, television, film, and stage. *Heroes* has been performed by theatres in the United States, England, and many other countries. His other plays include *Wheat City, The Medicine Line, Cruel Tears* -- a country opera in collaboration with Humphrey and the Dumptrucks, *The Shipbuilder, Gone the Burning Sun,* and *The Great Cultural Revolution*. Mitchell teaches English at the University of Regina.

AUTHOR'S INTRODUCTION

Heroes is not only a satire based on Superman and the Lone Ranger but is a study of heroes in crisis. Each of these characters has grown beyond the two-dimensional comic book and suffers the impact of the "real" world. This world has aged them, changed them, and now forgotten them. The heroes also discover that their former side-kicks --Tonto and Lois Lane -- have become the new heroes.

We may laugh to see the Lone Ranger and Superman ridiculed, but we cannot help feeling sympathy for these heroes in their decline. The playwright asks all the questions which we ignore when reading the comics, and gradually reveals how sheltered from reality these super-heroes are.

Do they represent the eclipse of the white male? Will the new heroes continue the relentless pursuit of justice. Tune in and find out.

Heroes is good light-hearted entertainment, but unlike the original comics, the play suggests that the emotions and pain are real.

Ken Mitchell

Heroes received its first professional production at the Globe Theatre, Regina, Saskatchewan in January, 1975 with the following cast:

LONE RANGER	*David Miller*
TONTO	*Stan Coles*
SUPERMAN	*Allan Strachan*
LOIS LANE	*Goldie Semple*

Directed by Esse W. Ljungh.

THE CHARACTERS

SUPERMAN
About 45, heavily built, but definitely over the hill. He has a slight paunch. Dressed in the full regalia. A city boy.

LONE RANGER
Slightly older, with a very deep voice. He is as tense as an over-wound mainspring, and exhibits a slight tremor in moments of crisis. Dressed in his crisp grey Western clothes, with white hat and black mask.

TONTO
An Indian, quiet and taciturn for the most part. He could be anywhere from forty to sixty. Dressed in buckskins.

LOIS LANE
Attractive, she carries her thirty-plus years well. Sharply dressed in career-woman clothing.

THE SET

The waiting room of an office, furnished in contemporary style, with an assortment of chairs and magazine tables. There is a glass-plated door at rear, with the word "CHIEF" on it. At right is the entrance from outside. At left is an open window, through which it can be seen that this office is in a rather tall building.

HEROES

SUPERMAN *is seated on a chair, his arms folded high on his chest, almost formally. A telephone rings three times inside the office.* SUPERMAN *turns, using his "x-ray" hearing to eavesdrop. But it is of no interest. He shakes his head, looks around the room, bored. He stretches, yawns, and suddenly leaps dramatically to his feet, flinging his cape back. He goes to the magazine table, flips perfunctorily through a couple of magazines, and throws them down again. He wanders about the room, makes a tentative leap in the air. Suddenly, for nothing better to do, he makes a great display of flexing his right bicep. While in this posture, he hears someone at the entrance, right, and leaps with a magnificent bound to his seat, resuming his heroic pose.*

The LONE RANGER *enters, looking tense and high-strung. He glances around quickly, looking for an ambush. There is only* SUPERMAN.

RANGER   *(touching his hat)* Afternoon.

SUPERMAN *ignores him, except for one flick of the eyes.* RANGER, *almost casually, checks his revolver, and sits down cautiously on the opposite side of the Chief's door. He suddenly seems very tired, tilts his hat back. He lifts his mask-like spectacles -- to rub his eyes. He sees* SUPERMAN *look at him, and quickly lowers the mask again. They sit silently.* RANGER *speaks finally.*

RANGER	It is not easy to stable a horse in downtown New York.
SUPERMAN	I suppose not.
RANGER	Take my advice.
SUPERMAN	Hm?
RANGER	Don't ever try it. Finally had to leave him in a parking lot. *(defensively)* Well, I couldn't just tie him to a parking meter, could I?
SUPERMAN	You can't leave him by himself?
RANGER	Certainly not.
SUPERMAN	Kinda stupid, is he?
RANGER	*(bristling)* Silver is not stupid!
SUPERMAN	A bit -- ornery?
RANGER	Do you mind if we change the subject?
SUPERMAN	Okay, okay! *(pause)* So -- you're in the horse business, huh?
RANGER	No, I am not in the "horse business."
SUPERMAN	What's with the weird costume, then?
	RANGER *looks at his clothes, then* SUPERMAN*'s, rather pointedly. He does not reply.*
SUPERMAN	Cows?
RANGER	No.
SUPERMAN	Sheep?
RANGER	No!

SUPERMAN	*(pause)* Pigs?
RANGER	No!
SUPERMAN	Sor-r-r-ry! *(pause)* It's a bit -- passe, isn't it? The boots and everything.
RANGER	All sorts of people wear clothes like this.

> RANGER, *getting irritated, snatches a magazine and snaps through a few pages. He is trying to think of a comeback.*

RANGER	May I ask what you're doing here?
SUPERMAN	Here?
RANGER	In this office.
SUPERMAN	*(curtly)* Business.
RANGER	What kind of business?
SUPERMAN	*(long pause)* What's the mask all about?
RANGER	Huh?
SUPERMAN	*(very clearly)* Mask?
RANGER	Are you trying to say you don't know?
SUPERMAN	*(pretending to think)* Batman!
RANGER	*(through clenched teeth)* Are you here on official business?
SUPERMAN	*(enjoying himself)* Who wants to know?
RANGER	The Lone Ranger wants to know!
SUPERMAN	*(pause)* Who?

RANGER

Lone Ranger! Lone Ranger! What the heck do you think this mask is for?

SUPERMAN

Oh, I dunno -- you see a lotta funny sights downtown these days.

> RANGER *leaps to his feet, snatches a couple of cartridges from his gun belt, pushes them in* SUPERMAN's *face.*

RANGER

Look! Look at these!

SUPERMAN

(non-commital) Interesting.

RANGER

Interesting? They're solid silver!

SUPERMAN

Some kind of dum-dums, are they?

RANGER

They're my own special bullets!

SUPERMAN

But why -- silver?

RANGER

(taken by surprise) Well, it's a kind of...trademark.

SUPERMAN

Oh. *(pause)* Oh! A horse called Silver! That mask! You're...

RANGER

(with some satisfaction) The Lone Ranger.

SUPERMAN

Right! A fiery horse with the speed of...

RANGER

Light!

SUPERMAN

Yeah. A cloud of dust and a hearty....*looking slyly at* RANGER*)...*Giddy-ap?

RANGER

(frostily) Hi-yo Silver, away!

SUPERMAN

Yeah, I remember now. *(shaking his head)* Man, that's a long time!

RANGER

What?

SUPERMAN   That musta been, what? Fifteen, twenty years... ?

RANGER   For your information, I've spent the last three
             weeks chasing a gang of desperate outlaws!

SUPERMAN   Train-robbers?

RANGER   *(pause)* Dope peddlers.

SUPERMAN   You don't say? *(friendlier)* Where's your, um,
             buddy?

RANGER   *(with the proper dignity)* I ride alone.

SUPERMAN   Oh, come on! Otto or whatever his...

RANGER   His name is Tonto.

SUPERMAN   Otto. Tonto. Pronto.

RANGER   And he is not my "buddy". He is my -- faithful
             Indian companion.

SUPERMAN   *(laughing)* He's what?

RANGER   You wouldn't understand. Easterners never do.

SUPERMAN   Whuddaya mean -- Easterner?

RANGER   *(not above sarcasm himself)* From -- the -- East.

SUPERMAN   Listen, pal. This might be a little hard for you to
             follow, but I've got a lot of territory to cover.
             (dramatic pause) I serve the world!

RANGER   The world?

SUPERMAN   Yeah -- the world.

                        Gestures a globe.

SUPERMAN   International.You know?

RANGER	*(suspiciously)* You sound like one of those anarchists.
SUPERMAN	*(incredulous)* What?
RANGER	You are implying there's something wrong with the good old U. S. of A., right?
SUPERMAN	Jesus. How long have you been out in Texas, anyway?
RANGER	Arizona.
SUPERMAN	Arizona.
RANGER	*(pause, with steely intent)* I believe we were discussing you.
SUPERMAN	Look, pal! I'm not wearing a mask! I got nothing to hide.
RANGER	How about that red cape? I suppose it represents something?
SUPERMAN	Represents?
RANGER	*(just getting warmed up)* Are you domiciled in this land of liberty and enterprise?
SUPERMAN	Huh?
RANGER	Do you live here?
SUPERMAN	Yeah, in a way.
RANGER	*(grimly)* You are evading my questions!
SUPERMAN	No, I'm not! I just -- well, I stay with a friend of mine. Clark Kent!
RANGER	You stay with a male friend?
SUPERMAN	Sort of. Clark is a reporter for...

RANGER	Male -- right?
SUPERMAN	Yes!
RANGER	And this little -- home of yours is in the East, right?
SUPERMAN	Jesus Christ! Is all this... ?
RANGER	Right?
SUPERMAN	...relevant?
RANGER	*(pause)* I could tell you were a fruit, the minute I laid eyes on that outfit.

> SUPERMAN *looks at his costume in surprise.*

RANGER	They'd laugh you out of every town west of the Mississippi.
SUPERMAN	They would not!
RANGER	Try it and see.
SUPERMAN	I been west of the Mississippi hundreds of times. Thousands of times!
RANGER	Did you take your -- friend along? Clark Kent?
SUPERMAN	Yes. No! He has to stay in -- Metropolis.
RANGER	Metropolis, eh?
SUPERMAN	He works there.
RANGER	I never heard of it.
SUPERMAN	*(trying hard)* You wouldn't have.
RANGER	*(pause)* Still, I will say it's...colourful.

SUPERMAN   What?

RANGER   Well, that bikini. The cape. The monogrammed shirt...

SUPERMAN   Monog...! That's my symbol!

RANGER   I see. "S" for symbol.

SUPERMAN   *(dangerously quiet)* Do you know that with a single breath, I could blow you right through that wall?

RANGER   Well, you've been doing your darndest for ten minutes now.

SUPERMAN   Do you realize that one blow from this -- fist of steel could send you into orbit around the moon?

RANGER   *(unimpressed)* A hazard I could learn to live with.

SUPERMAN   You're starting to piss -- me -- off!, fella!

RANGER   *(satisfied with his victory, standing up to ease the tension)* Have you been waiting here long?

SUPERMAN *refuses to answer.*

RANGER   *(cajoling)* Aw, come on. There's no point in sulking. If we gotta water at the same trough, we might as well pretend to be neighbourly.

SUPERMAN   Do you mind laying off the hillbilly metaphors?

RANGER   Pardon?

SUPERMAN   Save it for your -- fans!

RANGER   Suit yourself. I was only trying to pass the time of day.

SUPERMAN   *(pause)* Fifteen minutes!

RANGER	Pardon?
SUPERMAN	I was waiting -- fifteen minutes!

> *Pause.*

RANGER	What did you mean about my fans?
SUPERMAN	Fans?
RANGER	You said -- save it for my fans.
SUPERMAN	*(bored)* Did I?

> *Pause. The telephone behind the Chief's door rings three times. SUPERMAN listens intently. RANGER tries to hear, too, but can't. SUPERMAN finally shakes his head in disgust.*

SUPERMAN	So where's your "faithful Indian companion"?
RANGER	Oh, he's out at the silver mine. He can't stand the East. Couldn't drag him here with a herd of mustangs.
SUPERMAN	Did you say silver mine?
RANGER	Yeah.
SUPERMAN	You guys own a silver mine?
RANGER	Yeah. That's where these come from.
SUPERMAN	You mean that's all you do with it?
RANGER	Do with what?
SUPERMAN	Man, do you know how much silver is worth these days?

> *This sends RANGER off into one of his standard speeches.*

RANGER	Oh, yes! I do know its worth. In fact, that material value which you attach to it is what we seek to destroy -- by constantly employing these shining bullets as weapons in the fight for justice, and for decency, and for freedom. *(stabbing the air)* By eradicating the root of all evil from existence, we will preserve our founders' heritage and ...
SUPERMAN	You don't have to tell me, pal. Ever since I got to this planet, it's been fight, fight, fight -- just to keep a little law and order.
RANGER	*(pleasantly surprised)* You mean -- you too are engaged in the eternal battle against evil and perversion?
SUPERMAN	*(modestly)* In my own little way.
RANGER	There aren't many of us left these days.
SUPERMAN	It gets lonely sometimes.
RANGER	*(pause, checking his watch)* Hope that parking lot attendant is reliable.
SUPERMAN	I wouldn't trust one with a stale sandwich.
RANGER	*(alarmed)* Maybe I better go check...!
SUPERMAN	Oh come on. Where's he going to go with a horse?
RANGER	*(agreeing)* Yeah. *(pause, a bit puzzled)* That's strange about the fans.
SUPERMAN	What is?
RANGER	That's what he said, too. "Save it for your fans."
SUPERMAN	Who?

RANGER *looks around cautiously,*
flicks his thumb at the Chief's door.

RANGER   Him.

SUPERMAN   He invited you here?

RANGER   Yes.

SUPERMAN   All the way from Texas?

RANGER   Arizona. He telephoned.

SUPERMAN *seems shaken by this; put*
out, distracted.

RANGER   What is it?

SUPERMAN   Oh, nothing. Nothing. *(pause, suddenly)* You
ever get -- premonitions?

RANGER   *(startled himself)* Premonitions? What about?

SUPERMAN   Well, I...dunno. *(pause)* Had a kinda funny thing
happen on the way over here -- from Metropolis.

RANGER   Like what?

SUPERMAN   I guess it was over -- Baltimore I happened to
look down, and there was this house on fire. In
the suburbs. There were all these people, a
family, screaming from the windows, so I
swooped down to help.

RANGER   *(too politely, not believing a word)* Oh?

SUPERMAN   There was a little baby! And an old guy, must
have been eighty! They wouldn't have stood a
chance!

RANGER   I suppose not. *(long pause)* What exactly do you
mean, you swooped down?

SUPERMAN	Well I was in a rush, see, flying over and...
RANGER	You were flying over.
SUPERMAN	Yeah, and all this smoke curling up. Man, I flew right through it.
RANGER	Let me get this straight. You were flying along in this balloon, or airplane or whatever, and you just happened to look down and see...
SUPERMAN	No, no! I was flying -- all by myself!

> RANGER *begins flapping his arms like a bird, and caws like a crow.*

SUPERMAN	You see I've had the power of flight since... *(turning to* RANGER*)* Okay, knock it off, hayseed! *(turning away)* Anyway, when I -- landed, they...all started to laugh. They said to -- kiss off. It was a big joke! What are you grinning at?
RANGER	Well -- flying! That's a bit far-fetched, isn't it?
SUPERMAN	No more than those goddamn silver bullets!
RANGER	Eh?
SUPERMAN	I don't expect some dumb cowboy to know this, but I -- am Superman!
RANGER	*(suppressing a laugh)* Who?
SUPERMAN	Superman!

> RANGER*'s laugh runs down in the silence.*

RANGER	All right -- "Superman", what are you doing in here? In my Chief's office?
SUPERMAN	Your Chief's office?

RANGER   Yes.

SUPERMAN   Say, how do you earn your money, anyway?

RANGER   Well, I don't...I mean, Tonto looks after that side of things. *(pause)* Probably makes a few bucks selling beadwork and -- stuff.

SUPERMAN   Beadwork, huh?

RANGER   Sure! There's good money in -- well, how do you make money? Put on some kind of -- flying circus?

SUPERMAN   Clark gets a good salary at the Daily Planet. It keeps us in groceries.

> *They lapse into silence. Suddenly* SUPERMAN *hears a noise at the door right.* TONTO *steps inside, glances at the two heroes, and moves to a seat closer to* SUPERMAN *his eyes lowered deferentially.* SUPERMAN *is curious.* RANGER *can only stare at* TONTO.

RANGER   *(deciding to ignore* TONTO*)* Tell me more about this...flying.

SUPERMAN   Huh? Oh -- nothing to it. You just sort of jump into the -- listen, isn't he supposed to be in Arizona?

RANGER   Could you show me? Maybe flutter around the room a bit?

SUPERMAN   *(glancing)* Well, it's kinda narrow. I usually start from a window or something.

RANGER   How did you pick it up?

SUPERMAN   Oh, I always -- that is, ever since I got here from Krypton, I could...

RANGER   Krypton?

SUPERMAN   The planet where I was born. That's where I got
                all my superpowers, and stuff.

RANGER   That where the suit came from?

SUPERMAN   Yeah! That's right!

                > TONTO *suddenly looks up, catches*
                > RANGER*'s eye.*

RANGER   *(quickly to SUPERMAN)* Could you fly out that
                window?

SUPERMAN   Jeeze, I dunno. What if he calls...? *(gesturing at
                Chief's door)*

RANGER   Oh, it'll be hours yet! Come on, I've never seen
                anybody fly! Just a bit!

SUPERMAN   *(pleased)* All right. *(going to window)* I'll just
                have a quick soar around that skyscraper over
                there.

RANGER   That's the spirit.

SUPERMAN   *(leaping to window sill)* You watching?

RANGER   You're darned right!

SUPERMAN   UP! UP! And away! *(leaping out)*

RANGER   *(without turning from the window)* What are you
                doing here?

TONTO   Telegram. *(looking at the floor)*

RANGER   What?

                > TONTO *hands him a telegram without*
                > *looking up.* RANGER *glances out the*
                > *window. Smiles and waves.*

RANGER	*(shouting)* That's fantastic! *(reading the telegram, looking quickly at Chief's door, then to* TONTO*)* He sent for you?
TONTO	Yes -- Kemo Sabay.
RANGER	*(with clenched teeth)* Don't call me that!
TONTO	Yes -- sir.
RANGER	I thought you were going to stay in the mine?

TONTO *shrugs.*

RANGER	Things are bad enough already, without you just taking off anytime you feel like .
SUPERMAN	*(reappearing at the window)* How was that?
RANGER	What? Oh! Oh, great! I've never seen anything like that before!
SUPERMAN	You should see it at night. *(modestly)* I kind of glow...
RANGER	*(his mind elsewhere)* Tremendous. Fantastic.
SUPERMAN	He didn't call me, did he?
RANGER	No, no...nothing.

SUPERMAN *sits down. An uncomfortable silence.*

RANGER	That was really extremely interesting.
SUPERMAN	Thank you. *(pause, looking at* TONTO*)* Does he get to shoot silver bullets, too?
RANGER	Certainly not!
SUPERMAN	But he does all the mining, right?

RANGER   Well -- not all by himself. *(pause)* We have a few
            Mexicans -- you know, immigrant labourers.

SUPERMAN   He oversees it, though?

RANGER   Uh, yes. *(long pause, with forced joviality, to*
            TONTO*)* How's everything at the mine?

TONTO   *(eyes still lowered)* Things fine -- Kemo Sabay!

RANGER   What?

TONTO   Things fine -- sir.

RANGER   Good, good. No problems with the workers,
            then?

TONTO   No, Kemo Sabay.

SUPERMAN   What's that he called you?

RANGER   Never mind!

SUPERMAN   Oh come on. What did he say!

RANGER   *(embarrassed)* Kemo Sabay.

SUPERMAN   I know, Kemo Sabay! What does it mean?

RANGER   In Commanche or -- Sioux?

SUPERMAN   Uh, Commanche.

RANGER   *(relieved)* "Faithful friend."

SUPERMAN   Yeah? That's kinda neat. *(pause)* What does it
            mean in Sioux?

RANGER   Nothing.

SUPERMAN   *(pause, turning to* TONTO*)* What does it mean?

TONTO   *(glancing at* RANGER*)* It mean -- big shit head.

> RANGER*'s fist slams down hard on the chair beside him.* SUPERMAN *laughs.* TONTO *gazes at the floor. Again tense silence, and* SUPERMAN *begins cracking his knuckles.*

RANGER   Do you have to do that?

> SUPERMAN *shrugs, stops.*

RANGER   *(blurting)* What does he want us here for?

SUPERMAN   Oh...could be almost anything. Never know with him.

RANGER   Well, I wish he'd get on with it!

SUPERMAN   Do you mind telling me what the mask is for?

RANGER   What do you think?

SUPERMAN   Hiding from someone?

RANGER   *(biting his words off)* It symbolizes the blindfold of justice.

SUPERMAN   *(although he doesn't)* I see.

RANGER   *(pause)* It started out so Butch Cavendish wouldn't recognize me. He and his gang thought they'd killed me in a treacherous ambush.

SUPERMAN   But they -- didn't.

RANGER   No. I was discovered, and nursed back to life by my faithful -- by him.

SUPERMAN   You must be pretty grateful, huh?

RANGER   *(glaring at* TONTO*)* Yes.

SUPERMAN   Well. That's some story. Lotta good old-fashioned ...

> SUPERMAN *suddenly stiffens, hearing something. There is a crackling from the intercom speaker above their heads.* SUPERMAN *and* RANGER *turn to it.*

WOMAN'S VOICE   Mr. Tonto, please.

RANGER   What?

SUPERMAN   Who?

VOICE   The Chief will now see Mr. Tonto.

RANGER   *(completely staggered)* Mister -- Tonto!?

> TONTO *has risen, and walks quietly to the door. He opens it, smiles enigmatically at* RANGER, *and enters the Chief's offce.*

RANGER   *(astounded)* Did you see that? Did you see that?

SUPERMAN   Yeah. Strange, all right.

RANGER   Strange! I knew there was something funny going on. I could feel it in my bones! *(striking his fist into his palm)*

SUPERMAN   Premonitions.

RANGER   What?

SUPERMAN   You're so naive, Ranger. You treat him like some kind of lackey. He's probably robbing you blind!

RANGER   Tonto? Nonsense! If I can't trust Tonto, who...? *(pause)* Say, do you know something I don't?

SUPERMAN   I know people, and let me tell you, times are changing. Can't trust your best friends any more.

RANGER *(cautiously)* You find that, too?

SUPERMAN It's true! Just last week, I caught Jimmy Olson with his hand up Lois Lane's skirt.

RANGER Who?

SUPERMAN Lois Lane? She's my -- well, that's another story. *(pause)* Let's just say, it's not the same old world anymore, buddy. Everybody's out to screw the other guy.

RANGER *(aroused)* You can say that again!

SUPERMAN Like those people at Baltimore. Laughing at me like that.

RANGER Do you know silver used to be a trademark of quality? Now they don't even put it in coins anymore. This mask used to mean something. Now people try to shoot me down in back alleys.

SUPERMAN Tch - tch - tch.

RANGER I go into a town to...clean out the gamblers, say... and all the citizens turn on me. On ME! Like I was some kind of varmint!

SUPERMAN Discouraging, isn't it?

RANGER Women don't talk to me anymore. They think I'm queer!

SUPERMAN It's a tough row to hoe, all right.

RANGER I used to think about getting married. You know -- settling down, near the mine somewhere. Now the saloon girls laugh when I go in for a good time.

SUPERMAN I know the feeling.

RANGER *(suddenly)* Do you have a girl friend?

SUPERMAN	What do you think?
RANGER	This...Lois girl, huh? Is she...nice?
SUPERMAN	Stacked!
RANGER	*(pause)* Do you...? I mean, does she...you know?
SUPERMAN	*(smugly)* Come on, pal. Surely you don't expect me to go into...
RANGER	No, no! Of course not.

> Pause, as SUPERMAN *basks in* RANGER*'s envy.*

RANGER	*(clearing his throat)* Listen, you don't suppose if I came over to -- Metropolis some weekend, you could...?
SUPERMAN	Line up one of her friends for you? Sure. Any time.
RANGER	Uh, well, I was thinking some night when you're...working...I might...if she...
SUPERMAN	WHAT?
RANGER	You know, if you sort of asked her first...just said you had this friend
SUPERMAN	No, I don't think so!
RANGER	It wouldn't hurt you to...
SUPERMAN	You don't know Lois!
RANGER	...go without your fun...
SUPERMAN	Look!
RANGER	...one weekend!?

SUPERMAN	Let's just drop it.
RANGER	*(pause)* I can get you a few silver bullets.
SUPERMAN	No!

> *Silence.* SUPERMAN *starts tuning in to the conversation inside the office. Suddenly there is a tap on the outer door, and* LOIS LANE *enters, smartly dressed.*

LOIS	Well -- Superman!
SUPERMAN	*(startled)* Oh...hi...Lois.
LOIS	Why didn't you tell me you were coming here? You could have given me a ride.
SUPERMAN	I didn't know myself. That is, I didn't know you were coming!

> LOIS *turns, really sees* RANGER *for the first time.*

LOIS	Who's the, uh...*(raising her eyebrows at* SUPERMAN*)* stranger?
SUPERMAN	Him?
LOIS	Yes, -- him.
SUPERMAN	Just a visiting cowboy. Anything happening at the Daily Planet?
LOIS	Not much. Perry's getting off on his ecology trip again. Clark was supposed to do something on noise pollution this afternoon, but the silly twerp didn't show up.
SUPERMAN	*(just remembering it)* He didn't?
LOIS	Clark Kent -- loser of the century.

SUPERMAN	*(defensively)* Oh, he's probably just...
LOIS	Just what?
SUPERMAN	You know Clark -- heh, heh -- wandering around with his head in the clouds.
LOIS	*(suspicious)* Head in the clouds? Is that some kind of riddle, Superman?
SUPERMAN	No, no! *(startled)* It's a -- figger of speech!
LOIS	Figure of speech, eh? Superman, you better get a grip on yourself, or you're going to end up some sort of poetry freak.
SUPERMAN	*(with a nervous glance at* RANGER*)* Please, Lois...
LOIS	You're not going to start all that about people not understanding again, are you? Good God -- at the mayor's press reception, too! I was never so embarrassed...
SUPERMAN	*(in anguish)* Lois! *(gesturing at the presence of* RANGER, *who is mesmerized by all this)*
LOIS	...in my whole life. *(gazing at* RANGER*)* Well -- hello.
RANGER	*(embarrassed)* Afternoon, ma'am.
LOIS	I'm dying for an introduction. --
SUPERMAN	Oh. Uh, Lois, I'd like you to meet -- the Lone Ranger.

> LOIS *rises, advances on* RANGER *seductively.*

SUPERMAN	Ranger, this is my, um -- Lois Lane.
LOIS	Hi.

> LOIS *extends her hand.* RANGER *rises,*
> *trying at the same time to lift his hat,*
> *bow, and shake her hand.*

RANGER　　　P-p-pleased to meet you, ma'am.

LOIS　　　Ma'am? *(turning to* SUPERMAN*)* Did you hear that? Ma'am!

SUPERMAN　　　Yeah, he's -- you know -- kind of...

LOIS　　　That's very good, mister. *(appraising him)* I hope you keep that one.

RANGER　　　It gives me...great p-p-p-pleasure...

LOIS　　　*(already turned back to* SUPERMAN*)* So what are we all doing here?

SUPERMAN　　　I dunno! He called me at the Daily Planet and asked me to come over at three-thirty.

LOIS　　　*(sharply)* Why were you at the Planet?

SUPERMAN　　　*(stunned)* Oh, he didn't call me at the Planet! He called you at the Planet! Didn't he?

LOIS　　　Yeah. But you said...!

SUPERMAN　　　I was...confused.

LOIS　　　*(peering at him)* Are you all right? *(pause)* Where did he phone you then?

SUPERMAN　　　*(carefully to himself)* Where did he phone me then?

> LONE RANGER *sits down again.*

LOIS　　　Yes.

SUPERMAN　　　It wasn't...at home -- because I have no home!

LOIS   *(sighing)* So we've been led to believe. *(pause)*
                Why does he wear that mask?

SUPERMAN   Oh, that's a long story.

LOIS   *(looking directly at RANGER)* I love long
                stories.

SUPERMAN   *(blurting)* Well, he was in this ambush a few
                years ago, see

LOIS   *(crossing to RANGER)* It sounds...fascinating.

RANGER   *(in agony)* Oh, it isn't -- really...

SUPERMAN   No, it isn't, Lois!

LOIS   That mask does something for you.

SUPERMAN   *(desperate)* Yeah, it hides his face!

LOIS   I'd love to get the exclusive story on that mask.

RANGER   Oh, I don't think I could...

LOIS   *(tracing her finger around its edges)* There aren't
                any -- scars under it, are there?

RANGER   N-n-n- *(clearing his throat)* no!

LOIS   Why don't you take it off? Show us all the
                mysterious countenance?

RANGER   Oh no, I can't! It's...against the rules!

                LOIS *laughs, a long, seductive, musical
                laugh driving* RANGER *against the
                back of his chair.*

                SUPERMAN *crosses his legs and looks
                the other way.*

LOIS	I like that! Self-discipline! *(turning deliberately to* SUPERMAN*)* Too bad more of us didn't have it.
SUPERMAN	*(blurting)* Ask him about the saloon girls!
RANGER	*(startled)* What?
SUPERMAN	Laughing at you! Remember?
LOIS	Saloon girls? What are you guys talking about?
RANGER	Listen, Superman. Don't get me riled or...
SUPERMAN	Or what?

> RANGER *stands up and adjusts his gun in his holster.*

RANGER	Or you'll learn the Lone Ranger isn't a man to cross.
SUPERMAN	*(laughing)* If you think those stupid bullets are going to have the slightest effect on me...
LOIS	Now wait a minute, fellas!
RANGER	Wait nothing! If that Bolshevik pinko bushwacker thinks he can just come in here and...
SUPERMAN	*(rising)* Now, I warned you, hillbilly, about throwing your weight around.
RANGER	Some guys have just got to have their mouths shut for them.
SUPERMAN	You better stand away from him, Lois.
RANGER	Don't use your girlfriend to hide behind.

> *The following three lines are spoken simultaneously.*

LOIS	Stop it! Both of you!
SUPERMAN	Lois!
RANGER	You Communist!

The antagonists glare, poised for action. The Chief's door suddenly opens. RANGER reacts by whipping out his gun and almost shooting.

SUPERMAN	Shh!

TONTO comes out with a new air of authority and confidence. He walks through the frozen group, regarding them curiously, especially RANGER with his gun. They all stare at him as he sits down.

WOMAN'S VOICE	Mr. Superman now, please.

SUPERMAN leaps with alacrity to the door, grins triumphantly at RANGER, chagrined at being left. There is a long silence. RANGER looks at TONTO, turns to LOIS.

RANGER	I don't -- like it.
LOIS	Don't like what?
RANGER	The way things are...*(glancing at* TONTO, *who smiles and salutes him with a touch of insolence)*...happening around here.
LOIS	Aw, don't let it get you down *(helpfully)* Change is a permanent condition of our society.
RANGER	*(vaguely)* Yeah -- I suppose. *(to* TONTO) What did he...say?

TONTO	He's going to tell you himself -- Kemo Sabay.
LOIS	What did he call you?
RANGER	*(snapping)* Let's not go into that.
LOIS	*(pause)* You know, I like that about you. Decisive! None of your liberal wishy-washyness.

> TONTO *laughs, inexplicably. A pause.*

LOIS	Are you in town for long?
RANGER	*(trying desperately to maintain a grip on the situation)* No, not long. *(pause)* I've got my horse outside.

LOIS	Was that your horse? In the parking lot?

> RANGER *nods apprehensively.*

LOIS	Wow, that's a -- beautiful horse! What do you call him?
RANGER	*(with a modest little grin)* Silver.
LOIS	*(thoughtfully)* Silver.
RANGER	*(hopefully)* You like the name?
LOIS	Weird name for a horse, isn't it?

> TONTO *chuckles, just loud enough to be audible.*

LOIS	So what kind of work do you do?
RANGER	Oh, mostly tracking down crooks. That line of thing.
LOIS	Like who, for example?

RANGER	*(with a quick glance at* TONTO*)* Well, this week I -- that is, we -- rounded up a dope peddling ring in Nebraska.
LOIS	Dope peddlers! What was it? Heroin?
RANGER	No, no -- marijuana.
LOIS	Grass? *(pause)* Big operation, huh?
RANGER	Well...it wasn't what you'd call...
TONTO	*(to himself, but quite distinctly)* Two hippies.
	Long pause. LOIS *examines* TONTO *rather thoroughly.*
LOIS	You wouldn't know it by looking at him, but he lacks backbone.
RANGER	*(surprised)* Tonto?
LOIS	Superman!
RANGER	Oh.
LOIS	The Big Bopper!
RANGER	*(not used to this sort of thing at all)* Really?
LOIS	It's all physical, you see. He's got this big hulk of a body, and thinks that makes him a man. Well, it doesn't, does it?
RANGER	*(very uncomfortable)* Mmm.
LOIS	Now you. You're different. I mean, you're no pansy, but you don't come in here doing handstands and push-ups. Chauvinist pig!
RANGER	Huh?

LOIS	Not you! Him! Thinks because he can leap over tall buildings, et cetera, the whole world's going to adore him!
RANGER	*(interested despite himself)* I see your point.
	TONTO *rises and walks to the window, looks out, wanders around the room during the following scene.*
LOIS	There are other things, more important things, you know.
RANGER	Sure.
LOIS	Like a little sympathy once in a while. Some honest emotion!
RANGER	Oh, right. Right!
LOIS	Any kind of honesty. *(sighing)* Sometimes I think he lives in a world of fantasy.
RANGER	*(protesting)* Oh, no!
LOIS	Not like you! Out there, riding horses! Catching outlaws! That's reality!
RANGER	*(a moment of pride)* Yeah.
	TONTO *laughs again.*
LOIS	What's with him?
RANGER	*(to* TONTO, *with muted belligerence)* What are you laughing at?
TONTO	*(directly)* Nothing -- Kemo Sabay.
LOIS	He called you that again! Who is he?
RANGER	My -- Indian companion.

> LOIS *and* TONTO *gaze at each other for some time.*

LOIS   *(finally)* Little personal things, too.

RANGER   Oh?

LOIS   *(confidentially)* How many of those costumes do you think he's got? With that big "S" on it? *(as RANGER shrugs)* One!

RANGER   How does he...change...?

LOIS   That's just it! He never takes it off. Ever! That's the same costume he had on when he arrived on this planet, and I don't mind telling you, it could do with a wash.

RANGER   Yeah, well, I always make sure I've got -- you know, extra...underwear and...

LOIS   You don't notice it sitting here, but let him carry you a few hundred miles in his arms.

RANGER   Mmm.

LOIS   I can still smell Lana Lang's perfume. On wet days.

RANGER   Gee.

> LOIS *edges closer to* RANGER, *almost forcing him off his chair.*

LOIS   And his personal hygiene!

RANGER   *(faintly)* His -- what?

LOIS   Just try sharing a bedroom with him!

RANGER   *(alarmed)* Why? Is there something... ?

LOIS   Oh no, there's nothing wrong with him. He's
              straight, all right.

RANGER   *(miserably)* Oh -- good...

LOIS   Too straight, if you ask me.

              LOIS *whispers in* RANGER's *ear, and
              indicates the length of* SUPERMAN's
              organ: about fifteen inches. Even
              TONTO *reacts, though quietly.*

RANGER   *(thoroughly impressed)* That's -- really
              something.

LOIS   *(scornfully)* I suppose you think that's
              everything.

RANGER   Well, um...

LOIS   There's such a thing as sensitivity, you know.

RANGER   Mmmm.

LOIS   It's like making love with a machine! Boy!
              "More powerful than a speeding locomotive".
              Hah!

RANGER   *(nervously)* Heh, heh.

LOIS   Faster than a speeding bullet!

              RANGER *fails to suppress an hysterical
              giggle.*

LOIS   That sums him up. Psssshhht!

              LOIS *and* RANGER *both break out
              laughing. So does* TONTO. *Suddenly
              the door opens.* SUPERMAN *is
              shocked, somehow sensing that they're
              laughing at him.*

> *After a pause,* SUPERMAN *slouches to a chair as far as possible from the others, and dumps himself into it. They all watch. It is clear something quite shocking has happened to him.*

LOIS   Well?

RANGER   What did he say?

> SUPERMAN *waves them off vaguely, too preoccupied to look up.*

WOMAN'S VOICE   Miss Lane, please.

LOIS   Wish me luck!

RANGER   *(staring at* SUPERMAN*)* Yeah -- good luck.

> LOIS *goes in. There is a general silence.* TONTO *goes to the magazines, deliberately selects "Harper's" or "New Yorker" , and returns to his seat to study it, as* RANGER *watches.*

RANGER   *(finally)* She's -- quite a girl!

SUPERMAN   Hmm?

RANGER   Miss Lane.

SUPERMAN   Oh -- yeah...

TONTO   Well, I wouldn't throw her out of bed!

> *A shocked pause.*

RANGER   What did you say?

TONTO   *(looking up from his magazine)* You didn't hear me -- Kemo Sabay?

SUPERMAN   *(without much conviction)* Look -- buddy. I could throw you out that window so fast ...

TONTO   Yes, I know. You're faster than a speeding bullet!

SUPERMAN   *(stunned)* What did you say?

TONTO   I didn't say it. Your -- girlfriend did.

SUPERMAN   *(to* RANGER*)* Did she?

RANGER   Yeah.

SUPERMAN   That...that...

TONTO   *(innocently)* Bitch?

SUPERMAN   Bitch!

RANGER   Oh, come on now...

SUPERMAN   Come on nothing! You know what that...that Jezebel did?

RANGER   It can't be as bad as all

SUPERMAN   To me! Superman! You know what she did?

                  RANGER *shakes his head.*

SUPERMAN   She's taken over!

RANGER   Taken -- over?

SUPERMAN   The whole goddamned works! Lock, stock and barrel!

RANGER   Took over what?

SUPERMAN   Do I gotta draw a picture? The comic books! The TV show! It's all gonna be Lois Lane from now on!

RANGER I don't get it!

SUPERMAN Lois Lane Comics! The Lois Lane Show! "With her friend -- Superman". Ohhhhh! *(rocking in his chair, on the verge of tears)* OHHHHHHH!

RANGER But that's impossible! She can't do that to...*(a horrible realization dawns on RANGER, as he looks at TONTO, who is taking a cigar case from his pocket and lighting a large cigar)* ... to a hero -- somebody who -- has so many fans and represents...*(trailing off into silence)*

SUPERMAN *(flailing himself with pity)* Well, she did. No -- that's not fair. He *(pointing at office)* did it. We have to be "relevant", he said. The bottom was dropping out of circulation. Too many women readers were complaining about me!

RANGER Readers -- complaining?

SUPERMAN People have "different expectations" now, he said. So he's giving Lois a new image. They're making her into a -- liberated woman!

RANGER A what?

SUPERMAN You know, a feminist! I knew Women's Lib was a gang of subversives! I should have smashed it when I had the chance.

TONTO *(almost sympathetically)* You couldn't have stopped it.

RANGER What do you know about this?

TONTO *shrugs.*

TONTO Plus ça change, plus c'est la meme chose.

SUPERMAN The forces of evil couldn't touch me with atom bombs and laser beams! It took a woman!

RANGER   *(his mind elsewhere)* Easy now; take it easy.

SUPERMAN   *(an anguished cry to the heavens)* What am I going to do?

RANGER   *(pause)* Listen -- um -- Tonto...?

TONTO   Yes -- Kemo Sabay?

RANGER   I've been thinking. That silver mine -- our silver mine -- has been producing pretty good lately. More than we actually need -- for bullets, that is -- and I was thinking...

TONTO   *(flicking his ash)* Fourteen tons in the last fiscal year.

RANGER   *(stunned)* What? Oh -- oh yes, that's what I mean, and -- well, we haven't had a good break for quite a while, and what would you think about -- well, a little vacation?

TONTO   *(thoughtfully)* A vacation?

RANGER   Yeah! We'll spend some of that silver for a change! *(with desperate enthusiasm)* We'll just take off! The two of us! Go down to Tijuana or -- or Acapulco! Drift along the beaches for a few days!

TONTO   Days?

RANGER   Oh, weeks! Months! We'll have ourselves a ball! Listen, we'll go drinking -- together! And find some girls. White girls!

TONTO   You know -- I've been thinking of a vacation, too.

RANGER   Fantastic! *(to SUPERMAN)* You see? Same wave length! We click together like that all the time!

TONTO	But I was thinking more of -- the Algarve. Or Majorca. Maybe the Canaries.
RANGER	Canaries?
TONTO	Yes. I own a couple of hotels there. *(with polite condescension)* Why don't you come with me? I'll give you the -- economy rate.
RANGER	*(trying to assimilate all this)* That sounds -- really fine, old buddy.
SUPERMAN	*(finally attentive)* Listen, you guys.
RANGER	*(heartily)* Good old Tonto! Always comes up with the winning idea!
SUPERMAN	You don't suppose I could...go along?
RANGER	*(deferentially)* What do you think, Tonto?
SUPERMAN	I could really use a holiday. I'm just a bundle of nerves.
RANGER	He's not a bad fellow, Tonto.
TONTO	I don't know.
SUPERMAN	I could fly you there! Both of you!
RANGER	How about it, Tonto?
SUPERMAN	Whuddaya say?
TONTO	*(pause)* Well...we'll see.
SUPERMAN	Thanks a lot, you guys! I promise, you won't be sorry you took me...
	The Chief's door opens and LOIS *strides confidently out.*
LOIS	Okay, big boy. Let's go.

SUPERMAN *rises uncertainly.*

LOIS

We've got a lot to do today.

SUPERMAN

A lot -- to do?

LOIS

(a busy woman) Yes, there's an oil spill off Cape Cod we have to investigate for The Planet. *(checking watch)* Then we'll fly over to Cleveland and expose a welfare scandal. If you're up to it.

SUPERMAN

Sure I feel up to it, Lois! I was just telling the fellas here how good I been feeling.

WOMAN'S
VOICE

Mr. Ranger, please.

RANGER *stands, begins crossing slowly to door.*

LOIS

(to TONTO*)* Do you get into town very often -- Tonto?

TONTO

Oh, the way things are now...

RANGER *halts, looks at him.*

TONTO

...probably once a week or so.

LOIS

(with a seductive smile) Give me a call the next time you're in.

TONTO

Love to.

SUPERMAN

(at her elbow) Say, uh, Lois -- I was talking to these guys about a little vacation, you know, and...

LOIS

Vacation? You must be joking.

SUPERMAN

It's a...matter of -- adjusting...

LOIS   *(waving him to the door)* Later, later! We're
                behind schedule.

SUPERMAN   *(in a pleading tone as he retreats)* So long, you
                guys. Don't -- forget now. I'll fly you!

                LOIS *pushes him out the door, turns
                and throws a last smile at* TONTO, *then
                exits.*

RANGER   *(at Chief's door)* Listen, uh, Tonto...do you
                think it's too late to...work out some kind of...?

TONTO   Good luck -- Kemo Sabay.

RANGER   *(hopelessly)* Thanks, Tonto -- Old buddy.

                RANGER *enters the office.* TONTO
                *exhales a stream of cigar smoke toward
                the ceiling, relaxing as he waits for*
                RANGER *to come out. As the lights
                begin to dim, he takes a handful of
                silver cartridges from his pocket and
                loads them into his revolver, chuckling
                to himself.*

TONTO   *(shaking his head in amusement)* Kemo Sabay!

                This breaks TONTO *up into a long,
                hearty laugh. He is still laughing and
                shaking his head as the stage goes to
                black.*

                The End.

MOON PEOPLE

AVIVA RAVEL

Aviva Ravel is a Montrealer who has written for stage, CBC Radio, and television. Her plays include *Dispossessed* , and *The Twisted Loaf* - peformed at the Saidye Bronfman Centre, *Soft Voices* and *Mendel Fish. My Rumanian Cousin* and *The Courting of Sally Schwartz* have run extensively in Montreal while the plays *Moving Out, Gently Down the Stream* and *Vengeance* are presented in repertory by Cameo Productions, a touring company.

Ravel is currently compiling a collection of monologues for the stage and published short stories entitled *Separate Pieces*. She holds a doctorate in Canadian Drama and teaches in the English Department of McGill University and College Marie-Victorin.

AUTHOR'S INTRODUCTION

Moon People is a drama that presents an encounter between a mother and the teen-age daughter she had given up for adoption at birth. Adoption is an emotionally-charged and complex issue, and the play neither attempts to justify or condemn the mother's decision, but to show how their respective lives have turned out. While we empathize with Harriet who had suffered a great deal in early childhood, we also understand Marilyn's dilemma and the social pressures of the time. What is important is that, as a result of their meeting, they understand each other better. The past cannot be altered, but now Harriet is able to undertake the most difficult task of all -- to put the past behind her and, with the help of her loving adoptive family, attempt to create a fulfilling life for herself.

Aviva Ravel

Moon People was first presented at the Quebec Drama Festival at Centaur Theatre in Montreal, April 26, 1988 with the following cast:

MARILYN   *Ann Page*
HARRIET   *Maxine Messer*

Direction and set design by Bob Pot.

The present version of *Moon People* was first presented by Cameo Productions at Wagar High School, Montreal, March 31, 1989 with the following cast:

MARILYN   *Susan Corbett*
HARRIET   *Alison Aylward*

Stage manager - Thelma Perlman.
Technical director - Paul Talley.
Directed by Aviva Ravel.

In subsequent performances the role of HARRIET was played by *Julie Luoma*.

THE CHARACTERS

MARILYN — An actress, aged 36, attractive, wears expensive clothes of good taste.

HARRIET — Aged 17. She wears jeans, sneakers, a jean jacket, leather belt, and a chain around her neck with rings and charms. Inside her jacket pocket, is a large penknife. She is slim, agile, and physically quite strong. We see many facets of her personality during the course of the play.

THE SCENE

A small area of a playground in a city park consisting of a bench, a trash can, see-saw or swing, and a small children's wading pool. OFF-STAGE: a ball park, other playground equipment such as swings, sandbox, slides, stretch of lawn. Occasionally we hear children's voices, passers-by, cars, and other typical of neighbourhood park sounds. The sounds diminish in the course of the play as it is late afternoon and the younger children leave the park with their parents.

THE TIME -- The present. Summer, late afternoon.

THE MUSIC

The play begins and ends with the lullaby "Mockingbird".

MOON PEOPLE

	MARILYN *sits on bench studying a manuscript.* HARRIET *enters. She holds a can of soda pop and speaks to a kid, off.*
HARRIET	Hey you, leave that kid alone. I'm talkin' to you. You wanna get your nose busted? Scram, get out of here...S'okay, kid, he won't bother you no more.
	HARRIET *addresses the woman who is absorbed in her manuscript.*
HARRIET	Can't stand bullies pickin' on little kids. *(approaching bench)* You mind?
MARILYN	*(glancing up momentarily)* Uh...no...
HARRIET	*(sitting)* Thanks. *(stretching her legs)* So, what's more perfect than a day in June?
MARILYN	Are you talking to me?
HARRIET	You see someone else on this bench?
	MARILYN *looks back into her manuscript.*
HARRIET	I asked what's more perfect than a day in June?
	MARILYN *turns a page.*
HARRIET	A day in autumn. It's still warm, the wind blows through your hair, and the leaves are changin' color. When you walk on them, it's like walkin' on rainbows. What's your favorite season?
	MARILYN *does not reply.*

HARRIET   Mine's summer, but I like winter too. Skatin' on
the ice, slidin' on toboggans, making snowmen.
Don't like spring. Y'never know what's gonna
happen. Sometimes it's cold, or it's hot, or it
rains, and y'get sick with flu...What's one of
your ten favorite things?

        MARILYN *annoyed by the disturbance,
tries to concentrate on her manuscript.*

HARRIET   Mine's watchin' kids playin' in the park. There's
one buildin' a castle in the sand. There's a cute
one with blonde curls and a fatty one with
freckles. And there's a daddy swingin' his kid up
in the air. *(swaying her body)* Up and down, up
and down, and all the Mommys push the
carriages back and forth, back and forth. *(to
MARILYN)* Nice uh?

        MARILYN *does not reply,* HARRIET
moves closer to her.

MARILYN   Look, Miss...

HARRIET   *(extending her hand)* Harriet Waller. Hi.

MARILYN   *(not taking her hand)* There are other benches
here. If you want this one, I'll move.

HARRIET   Please don't. It's an honor to sit beside you,
Marilyn Perkyns.

MARILYN   *(surprised)* You know who I am?

HARRIET   Sure. I'm a fan.

MARILYN   Really?

HARRIET   Saw you in *The Doll's House.*

MARILYN   You did?

HARRIET	*(pleased with herself)* Surprised you, uh? Also saw you in...that play about three rotten people trapped in hell and they can never get out.
MARILYN	*No Exit.*
HARRIET	Yeah, that's it. You always play people being trapped.
MARILYN	It seems so.
HARRIET	I don't believe there's such a place like hell 'cause it's so bad right here. If it was good here all the time, I suppose there might be a hell, but if everybody was good, nobody would go there so you wouldn't need it. So nobody believes in hell 'cause if they did everybody would be good cause they'd be afraid to go there. You get what I mean?
MARILYN	*(amused by the girl, but her manuscript takes precedence)* As much as I'd like to talk to you, I'm very busy now, so if you'll excuse me...
HARRIET	Truth is I never saw you in those plays.
MARILYN	Oh?
HARRIET	My Mom told me what they're about 'cause I got no patience to read the papers.
MARILYN	I see.
HARRIET	She says you re a pretty good actress. Not like Elizabeth Taylor, but pretty good.
	MARILYN *tries to concentrate on her manuscript.*
HARRIET	You learnin' lines from a play?
MARILYN	I'm trying to.

HARRIET	*(looking at manuscript)* The Silver Cord. What's it about?
MARILYN	Look, Miss Waller, I told you I'm busy.
HARRIET	Come on, tell me, and I won't bother you no more.
MARILYN	It's about a mother who's so attached to her sons she can't let them go.
HARRIET	*(grinning)* Trapped again.
MARILYN	One gets away.
HARRIET	He breaks the cord?
MARILYN	Symbolically.
HARRIET	Ah, it's not a real cord.
MARILYN	It refers to the umbilical cord.
HARRIET	Ah...if they didn't cut the cord you could be with your mother forever. *(laughing)* All those people attached to their mothers, walkin' down the street, one wants to go to the supermarket, one wants to go to a movie, and they pull and fight and get all tangled up. If a mother has five kids and the five kids grow up, and they each have five kids, that would be some big tangle!
	MARILYN is both amused and annoyed at the interruption, but is somehow drawn to the girl.
MARILYN	Yes.
HARRIET	But it ain't that way at all. After they cut the cord, the mother can say: "I don't want you, baby, so get lost."
MARILYN	People don't do that.

HARRIET	Don't they?
MARILYN	*(uneasy, looking intently at her script)* No.
HARRIET	You playin' the mother?
MARILYN	Yes.
HARRIET	That's a good part for you. You look like a nice mother. Are you? A nice mother, I mean?
MARILYN	I hope so.
HARRIET	Well, looks don't mean nothin'. A person may look nice, all dressed up and smiling, but he may be stinkin' like a sewer inside.

> HARRIET *has finished her soda pop, tosses the empty container into the garbage can, then looks inside.*

HARRIET	One'f my ten favourite things is lookin' in the garbage. Y'can tell a lot about people from their garbage. There are two kinds of people -- thrower-outers and savers. What are you?
MARILYN	I beg your pardon?
HARRIET	Do you like to throw things out or save them?
MARILYN	I throw things out when I don't need them anymore.
HARRIET	That figures. Me, I don't throw nothin' out. My Mom calls my room the city dump...I also keep things in my head forever. Do you?

> MARILYN *does not reply.*

HARRIET	Bet you don't. Soon's somethin' happens, you forget, uh?
MARILYN	You said you wouldn't bother me anymore.

HARRIET	I didn't swear, so it don't count. *(looking into the garbage can)* Beer-drinkers, potato chipeaters, teddy bear, a ball, and a good skipping rope. *(stuffing an old shoelace into her pocket, leaning the teddy bear against the garbage can, then skipping rope)* One two, buckle my shoe, three four, shut the door. Pepper!

> HARRIET *abruptly stops jumping, and on "Pepper" hits the bench dangerously close to* MARILYN *who is startled.*

HARRIET	Scared you, uh? Don't worry, I ain't gonna hurt you.

> MARILYN *rises and starts toward exit.*

HARRIET	Where you goin'?
MARILYN	That's none of your business.
HARRIET	*(blocking her way)* To the theatre, huh?
MARILYN	Would you please let me pass.
HARRIET	Every day you go to the theatre at 5:00. But the play opens tonight, so you don't have to be there till 7:00.
MARILYN	Have you been following me?
HARRIET	Yeah. But I never had the nerve to talk to you till now.
MARILYN	What exactly do you want?
HARRIET	Uh...your autograph.
MARILYN	Alright.

> HARRIET *takes a notepad and pencil out of her pocket and hands it to* MARILYN.

HARRIET	Write "To Harriet with love."

MARILYN *writes.*

HARRIET	Thanks a lot. *(reading)* "To Harriet with love, Marilyn Perkyns". This is incredible! Your handwriting is a lot like mine. You wanna see?
MARILYN	No. Now if you'll excuse me....
HARRIET	Stay right where you are, Mrs. Perkyns!
MARILYN	Will you please get out of my way!
HARRIET	You ain't goin' nowhere. Not till I say so.
MARILYN	What do you want?
HARRIET	To talk to you.
MARILYN	I don't want to talk to you.
HARRIET	Sure you do.
MARILYN	Please let me pass!
HARRIET	Sit down!
MARILYN	Get out of my way!
HARRIET	I told you to sit down!
MARILYN	I'll call the police.
HARRIET	*(reaching into her jacket pocket)* I wouldn't if I was you. *(gripping MARILYN's arm)*
MARILYN	Let me go!
HARRIET	I got a knife, see? Very sharp. One stab through the heart and you're dead. Or maybe I 'll mess up your pretty face, uh?

MARILYN	*(frightened)* You want my purse, take it. I only have twenty dollars.
HARRIET	Don't want your money. Just sit down!

> MARILYN, *tense and nervous, sits.*

HARRIET	That's better. Now -- gimme your bag.

> MARILYN *hands over her purse.*
> HARRIET *examines the contents,*
> *withdraws a wallet, opens it and looks*
> *at photographs.*

HARRIET	These your kids?
MARILYN	Yes. *(making a move to retrieve the wallet)*
HARRIET	Don't worry, I wont eat 'em. Who's this cute one?
MARILYN	Henry.
HARRIET	*(turning photo over)* Yeah. And this one is...
MARILYN	Arthur.
HARRIET	What d'you call 'im. Artie? Artsie? *(turning photo over)* Art, June 1983. He's a serious type, uh? What does he do? Play the violin?
MARILYN	The piano.
HARRIET	Is that so? This must be the baby with the fat face. What d'you call him?
MARILYN	Gordon.
HARRIET	*(looking at other side)* Wrong. Dondee. My Mom calls me "Harry". When I do somethin' real nice, she calls me "chocolate chip" and kisses my elbow.

MARILYN	Your elbow?
HARRIET	Some bitch broke my arm when I was a kid, so I got this crooked elbow. My Mom kisses it to take the pain away, even though it don't hurt no more.
MARILYN	I see.
HARRIET	So you got three boys, no girls?
MARILYN	No.
HARRIET	Didn't you never want a girl? A pretty one to wear dresses and ribbons?
MARILYN	Of course, but...
HARRIET	Maybe you'll get lucky and have a girl some day. No picture of your husband? Whatsamatter, you don't like him?
MARILYN	Of course I like him. I just don't carry his photo.
HARRIET	He probably don't carry yours neither.
MARILYN	He keeps one of me on his desk.
HARRIET	*(amused)* Is that so? I don't think you like him so much. You can always tell by the smile. Women with big smiles got nice husbands. You don't smile big. Bet he's rich though.
MARILYN	We're not poor.
HARRIET	What kind'f rip-off business does he do?
MARILYN	He doesn't rip off anyone.
HARRIET	My Dad says anyone rich is ripping off someone else. He says someday there ain't gonna be no poor people and nobody's gonna go round scarin' kids and breakin' their arms. So, you got a lover?

MARILYN	No!
HARRIET	Come on, I won't tell nobody. All actresses got lovers. You read that in *People* magazine.
MARILYN	I don't have a lover.
HARRIET	I guess you're not so famous.
MARILYN	Please give me my bag. I really have to go!
HARRIET	When I'm good and ready.
MARILYN	Right now!
HARRIET	You want these pictures, uh? Here's one.

> HARRIET *tears it up and lets the pieces drop to the ground.*

MARILYN	Stop that!
HARRIET	*(tearing the second photo)* And another.
MARILYN	Give me my bag!
HARRIET	And here goes the baby. *(tearing it too)* Don't feel so bad, you can take more more pictures. You like those boys, uh? They never give you no trouble?
MARILYN	No!
HARRIET	I give my parents lots of trouble. Stay out till four in the morning, come home stoned and drunk. Once I made such a racket the cops chased me down the street, woke up the whole neighbourhood. Lots of times I spent the night in jail. The cops treat me okay. They give me coffee in the morning. They call me juvenile delinquent. Bet your boys never seen the inside of a jail.

MARILYN   You want to keep my bag, all right. Just let me
           have the keys. *(trying to retrieve her bag)*

HARRIET   Sit down!

                    MARILYN *resumes her seat on bench.*

HARRIET   One of my ten favorite things is lookin' in
           people's bags. It's like garbage. Tells you
           everything about a person.

                    HARRIET *sits on edge of pool,
                    removes items from bag.*

HARRIET   Mirror, nail file, lipstick, shadow, mascara -- me,
           I don't use that stuff. Receipt from cleaners.
           Why don't the maid pick up the clothes?

MARILYN   It's not her job.

HARRIET   She does the cleaning and makes the dinner, uh?

MARILYN   Yes.

HARRIET   My Mom would be real jealous. She ain't crazy
           about cleaning and cooking. You eat with
           candlesticks?

MARILYN   Sometimes.

HARRIET   You at one end, the husband at the other, and the
           three cutsie boys all around, uh?

MARILYN   Yes.

HARRIET   My Mom and Dad sit next to each other.
           Sometimes they hold hands under the table, that
           makes us all laugh. So what's his name, the
           husband's?

MARILYN   It's none of your business.

HARRIET	You're gonna tell me in the end anyhow, so you may as well do it now. So what's his name?
MARILYN	Charles.
HARRIET	Like the prince, uh? Real classy. My Dad's name is Abraham. We call him Abe. Your husband's got hair?

     MARILYN *nods.*

HARRIET	My Dad don't got any cause he's smart. The more brains a person has, the less hair. That's how it works.

     HARRIET *has moved to the bench*
     where she examines more items from
     MARILYN's *purse.*

HARRIET	So many credit cards.

     MARILYN *makes a move to retrieve*
     them.

HARRIET	Don't worry I don't want them. Perfume. Smells nice. Used to rip these off at the stores and sell 'em half price. I'll keep it for a souvenir. *(slipping it into a pocket)* Phone bill. You talk a lot long distance. Who d'you talk to?
MARILYN	It's none of your business.
HARRIET	Your lover?
MARILYN	My mother.
HARRIET	You shouldn't talk to her so much, she's a witch.
MARILYN	Why do you say that?
HARRIET	She scared you a lot when you were a kid. You got a scared look in your eyes.

MARILYN   I'm not scared.

HARRIET   You were when you thought I'd knife you.

MARILYN   Anyone would be frightened. Now may I please
                 have my bag?

HARRIET   Take it.

                 HARRIET *shoves the bag at*
                 MARILYN *who moves to side of pool*
                 and replaces the items HARRIET *had*
                 taken out .

HARRIET   You're very ordinary, nothing special. No secret
                 letters, no hash, not even Alka Seltzer. Don't
                 you get upset stomach?

MARILYN   No.

HARRIET   Heartburn?

MARILYN   No.

HARRIET   You have a scalp condition?

MARILYN   No!

HARRIET   Athlete's foot?

MARILYN   No!

HARRIET   You wear contact lenses?

MARILYN   No.

HARRIET   You got sicknesses like asthma?

MARILYN   No!

HARRIET   If you mind about the perfume, you can have it
                 back.

MARILYN	Keep it.
HARRIET	You're generous, like me.
MARILYN	May I go now?
HARRIET	Nope.
MARILYN	How long is this going to take?
HARRIET	Depends. Sing me a lullaby.
MARILYN	Sing? Here?
HARRIET	You're not shy, are you? You're an actress.
MARILYN	Very well... "Hush little baby don' t say a word, Mama's gonna buy you a mockingbird".
HARRIET	*(pulling her to the bench)* Wait wait, first I gotta lie in your lap.

> HARRIET *lies on bench, puts her head on* MARILYN*'s lap.*

HARRIET	Now sing, like you mean it, like I was your baby.
MARILYN	"Hush little baby don't say a word, Mama's gonna buy you a mockingbird. If that mockingbird don't sing, Mama's gonna buy you a diamond ring..."
HARRIET	Stroke my hair, go on, you see it's nice and soft. You sing nice. My Mom sings like that to keep the nightmares away. About weird men with claws burning me all over. When she sings the Moon People come out and the nightmares go away. The Moon People are good. We play games and talk about beautiful birds and tall mountains.

> HARRIET *sits up.*

HARRIET	You ever think of going to the moon?
MARILYN	No.
HARRIET	You got no imagination.
MARILYN	Please let me go now. I have to get into my costume.

> MARILYN *tries to retrieve her keys which are in* HARRIET's *possession, but* HARRIET *holds on to them.*

HARRIET	You nervous about the play?
MARILYN	A little.
HARRIET	Suppose you forget your lines and the play don't turn out like it's supposed to.
MARILYN	That doesn't happen.
HARRIET	In real life things don't turn out like they're supposed to.
MARILYN	In a play, everything is planned.
HARRIET	If you know what's gonna happen there's no excitement.
MARILYN	The audience doesn't know.
HARRIET	If they read the play, they do.
MARILYN	Then they enjoy the acting.
HARRIET	I'd like to be an actress, but I'm too shy.
MARILYN	I never would've known. *(appealing to her)* I really have to go now. Maybe I can see you later. I'll get you a ticket for the show.

HARRIET	Never mind the show. Real life is more exciting. *(returning keys to her pocket)*
MARILYN	Please, Harriet...
HARRIET	I like when you say my name. It wasn't always Harriet. It used to be Janice, but my Mom changed it.
MARILYN	*(taken aback)* Janice?
HARRIET	Yeah, you know somebody called Janice?
MARILYN	*(uneasy)* No.
HARRIET	I know somethin' about you practically nobody else does.
MARILYN	What's that?
HARRIET	A big secret.
MARILYN	Is that so?
HARRIET	You look scared again. Don't worry, I don't do blackmail.
MARILYN	What's the big secret?
HARRIET	Guess.
MARILYN	I can't.
HARRIET	Sure you can. Everybody's got somethin' to hide.
MARILYN	I don't know what you're talking about.
HARRIET	Liar! Your name used to be Marilyn Evans. On August 13, 1972, you were at the Hillside General Hospital. You gave birth to a baby girl. She weighed eight pounds, nine ounces. That's the secret.

MARILYN	Oh, my God!
HARRIET	I told you real life is more exciting than your play.
MARILYN	Who are you...
HARRIET	Tell me about the baby. Was she pretty? Did it take long to give birth? Did it hurt a lot?
MARILYN	Are you...
HARRIET	Did you nurse her a little, did you hold her? Did you cry when you gave her away?
MARILYN	It can't be...
HARRIET	Don't you recognize me?
MARILYN	You are...
HARRIET	Maybe yes, maybe no. What do you think?
MARILYN	I...I don't know.
HARRIET	I thought after I found you, you'd grab me and hug me. "My child! My long lost child." Like in the fairy tales. But all you can say is "I don't know." Well, you do know.
MARILYN	*(pause)* How did you find me?
HARRIET	Then it is you! I knew it! I could tell! I'm glad you're so pretty.

MARILYN *stares at her, still shocked.*

HARRIET	You're sorry it's me. You wished if I turned up I'd be polite and brainy, never in trouble, you're disappointed, eh?
MARILYN	No...

HARRIET   You *are* sorry.

MARILYN   No. I'm just...surprised.

HARRIET   You never expected me to turn up, uh?

> HARRIET *sits on bench.*

MARILYN   No.

HARRIET   So how come I was born? Bet I wasn't planned or anything.

MARILYN   No.

HARRIET   Who was the father? Were you raped or what?

MARILYN   Oh my God...

HARRIET   Well?

MARILYN   *(shaken)* I...I was away at college. I was in love with a student. When I told him I was pregnant, he left me.

HARRIET   That's it?

> MARILYN *nods.*

HARRIET   You sure it was him? Maybe you slept around.

MARILYN   I didn't.

HARRIET   I don't neither. So, why didn't you have an abortion?

MARILYN   By the time I told him, it was too late.

HARRIET   You thought he'd stick by you, so you didn't tell.

MARILYN   Yes.

HARRIET   What was he studying?

MARILYN	Medicine.
HARRIET	Oh, a doctor! So he's very smart. What's his name?
MARILYN	What difference does it make?
HARRIET	It won't do you no good to be stubborn. You better tell me.
MARILYN	*(upset, as the memories are revived)* Howard.
HARRIET	Where's he from?
MARILYN	Boston.
HARRIET	You were sorry he left you?
MARILYN	Yes.
HARRIET	You're still sorry?
MARILYN	No.
HARRIET	Sure you are. I could tell by the way you said his name.
MARILYN	Sometimes.
HARRIET	So how come you abandoned me?
MARILYN	You weren't abandoned. The Agency told me you were adopted by a good family.

HARRRIET *laughs.*

MARILYN	What's so funny?
HARRIET	*(rising from bench)* You wanna know what really happened? The woman that took me died when I was eighteen months. Her husband didn't wanna keep me, so he gave me back.

HARRIET	Like you buy somethin' in the store and you change your mind, so you give it back, if you got a receipt.
MARILYN	Oh no!
HARRIET	*(mimicking her)* Oh yes.
MARILYN	So, what happened?
HARRIET	You really wanna know.
MARILYN	Yes.
HARRIET	You don't wanna go to your play now, uh?
MARILYN	No.
HARRIET	I told you real life is more exciting.
MARILYN	So what happened?
HARRIET	*(moving to wading-pool area)* I screamed everywhere they put me. Like fourteen places or so. Nobody would keep me. Would you've taken me back if you knew?
MARILYN	I couldn't. I was very young. My mother said she'd throw me out. I had nowhere to go...
HARRIET	She was ashamed for the neighbours and relatives. My Dad does what he thinks is right and he don't care about the neighbours.
MARILYN	I wanted to keep you, but I couldn't.
HARRIET	Wrong. You didn't want to hard enough. Maybe you were busy becomin' an actress. Too busy to look after me.
MARILYN	I thought you were all right, I tried to forget.
HARRIET	Did you?

MARILYN	I tried not to think about it.
HARRIET	So you liked me a little, you felt sorry.
MARILYN	Yes. I cried for months. You were a beautiful baby.
HARRIET	I was?! You got a picture?
MARILYN	No.
HARRIET	Shit! Nobody took pictures when I was a baby. But you got lots'f pictures of your boys. *(picking up scraps of the torn photos)*
MARILYN	Yes.
HARRIET	Everytime they did somethin' cute you took a picture, uh?
MARILYN	Yes.
HARRIET	It would be nice to have one when I was a baby, so when I got my own kids I could say: "You see, you look just like me." That's why I wanted to find you. Every person knows where his grandparents come from, I don't know nothing. Like if there's asthma in your family. Maybe my great-grandfather invented toasters...Did you ever walk down the street and wonder if any of the kids was yours?

> HARRIET *has dropped the photo scraps on the ground.*

MARILYN	Yes I did.

HARRIET	I used to do that a lot. I'd see a nice woman and ask: "Are you my mother?" Like that kids' book my Mom used to read to me. "The bird asked the horse: 'Are you my mother?' And the horse said: 'No'. The bird asked the cow: 'Are you my mother?' And the cow said: 'No'. The bird asked the bulldozer: 'Are you my mother?' And the bulldozer said: 'No.' At last he came to a big bird and he asked, 'Are you my mother?' And the bird said: 'Yes'." Only that never happened to me.

> HARRIET, *at the edge of the wading pool, removes her shoes, steps inside.*

MARILYN	*(moving toward her)* I'm sorry. I'm so sorry.
HARRIET	That's the easy part. *(fingering the water)*
MARILYN	What do you mean?
HARRIET	Take your shoes off, put your feet in the water and I'll tell you all about it.
MARILYN	I'd rather not.
HARRIET	Afraid you'll get your pretty dress dirty?
MARILYN	No.
HARRIET	So take off your damn shoes. How can you walk on those high heels anyway? Take 'em off.

> MARILYN *complies.*

HARRIET	Now sit beside me, over here. And I'll tell you the whole story.

> HARRIET *splashes water on her.*

HARRIET	Water's nice and warm, feels good, uh?
MARILYN	Stop that.

HARRIET	Don't get so excited. It's only water. It ain't gonna hurt you. So, you really wanna know what happened, eh?
MARILYN	Yes.
HARRIET	Everywhere they put me I screamed: Mommy, Mommy! Once they gave me to a big man with a red face. His wife had grey hair and wore a big dirty apron. When I screamed, he came at me with a big stick: "Your Mommy's dead, and she ain't comin' back, never. You scream once more you'll get it with this stick, and you'll be dead too." I never screamed again. Never talked neither. Never cried or laughed. They thought I was a retard.
MARILYN	Oh my God.

> *During following,* HARRIET *moves around the pool.*

HARRIET	One night this man was sittin' with guys drinkin' and playin' cards. It was a small room and it smelled bad. He made a bet that no matter what he did to me, I wouldn't cry. It was a game he played with me. When he hurt me and I didn't cry, he gave me presents. So he took off my shirt, and everyone put dollars on the table. He lit a cigarette and burned me all over. It hurt real bad but I didn't cry. He burned me twenty times, maybe more, then I fainted. I don't remember nothin' after that, just the woman puttin' stuff on the burns, and it hurt like crazy but still I didn't cry. And the man gave me a doll with a blue dress and yellow hair. But I never forgot the burnin'. So one day I ripped up the doll, tore her hair out, ripped the dress, and threw it in the garbage. I was sorry after 'cause I liked the doll. I was four years old.
MARILYN	*(horrified)* How awful...

HARRIET	How awful? Like *this* awful?!
	HARRIET *pulls* MARILYN *into the water and dunks her.*
HARRIET	Wanna see the scars? Look. *(baring her arm)* There's lots more on my back. Everytime I wear a swim suit, people think I got chicken pox. *(pause)* The woman in that place wasn't nice neither. I was drawin' a picture with a red house and orange sun and she came over and tore the picture and twisted my arm till it broke. I never figured out why she did it. It was a nice picture. *(pause)* So what do you think now? Should I drown you or what?
MARILYN	I didn't know!
HARRIET	You should've checked it out, but you didn't care.
	HARRIET *dunks her and pulls her up.*
MARILYN	They wouldn't have told me!
HARRIET	And suppose they did? Wouldn't've made no difference anyhow! You didn't give a shit about me
MARILYN	I did. Honestly I did! *(now sitting at edge of the pool)*
HARRIET	Then the social worker put me in the rejects place, with all the kids nobody wants to adopt. I was so screwed up, nobody looked at me twice. They thought I was weird. I wouldn't talk, just stared with my spooky eyes. But I fooled them. All the time I wasn't really there. I was in another place.
	HARRIET *slips on her shoes then lies down at the edge of the pool.*
MARILYN	What do you mean? Another place.

HARRIET	Lyin' on a beach all day, with the colors'f the rainbow dancin' in my eyes. The water comes into shore, playin' water music. Then a big golden bird flies down. I jump on its back and we go away above the clouds, over the mountains till we come to the Moon-People. I can stay there forever, where nobody is never sad or hungry, and everything is like a story with a happy ending.
MARILYN	Sounds like a nice place.
HARRIET	*(jumping up)* There ain't no such place! A person's got to live where it's real, not like you, in a play, but right here!

HARRIET *holds* MARILYN*'s arm.*

HARRIET	So, there I was hurtin' all over and goin' nuts while you were decoratin' your Christmas tree, and buyin' birthday presents for your boys, and takin' them on picnics! Right?!

HARRIET *slaps* MARILYN*'s face.*
MARILYN *sinks to the bench and weeps.*

HARRIET	Oh, I'm sorry, I didn't mean it. You all right? Look all the makeup is dripping.

HARRIET *hands* MARILYN *a tissue from her pocket,* MARILYN *dries her face.*

HARRIET	You don't need no makeup. You're pretty without it...You'll dry up soon. I got a terrible temper. I'm sorry.
MARILYN	Harriet, I know you're angry. I don't blame you, I wanted to keep you, but I couldn't.
HARRIET	You didn't even try.

MARILYN	Alright, I made a mistake. I'm sorry about what happened. Maybe now that you found me...
HARRIET	Yeah?
MARILYN	I could make it up to you.
HARRIET	How?
MARILYN	I'll -- take you home with me. I'll give you everything you want.
HARRIET	No kidding.
MARILYN	I *am* your mother.
HARRIET	Suppose your husband don't like the the idea.
MARILYN	He will. He's a good person.
HARRIET	No he ain't. If he was, you would've told him about me. You got tears in your eyes 'cause I'm tellin' the truth. Bet you don't even love him.
MARILYN	I do.
HARRIET	Not like you loved Howard. The first love is always the best. So, looks like you got a crummy life.
MARILYN	I'm okay.
HARRIET	No, you're not. Why did you marry him?
MARILYN	It was easier than living at home.
HARRIET	Tell me, how it was with you and Howard.
MARILYN	We were in love. Everything was beautiful. I thought it would last forever. We used to laugh a lot. You know we invented a secret language. And we'd talk to each other when other people were around. Everyone thought we were crazy.

HARRIET   How did it go?

MARILYN   I-pie a-pam gl-pad y-pou c-pame to-poo s-pee m-pee.

HARRIET   What's that mean?

MARILYN   I'm glad you came to see me.

HARRIET   Teach it to me.

MARILYN   You put a "p" between the syllables -- I-pie a-pam gl-pad y-pou.

HARRIET   *(completing the sentence)* c-pame t-poo s-pee m-pee.

MARILYN   That's it.

HARRIET   You're okay.

MARILYN   Thanks. So are you.

HARRIET   If Howard came back and wanted you, would you go with him and take me, and we'd be a family?

MARILYN   *(moving to see-saw)* I have another family now. I don't mean it like that.

HARRIET   I know what you mean. You have lots of good stuff and you don' t wanna take chances -- like your boys, and acting. Why do you act?

      The following can take place on the see-saw, they sit on either end and go up and down.

MARILYN   On stage I can laugh and cry and feel things.

HARRIET   Otherwise you don't feel things?

MARILYN   Sure I do.

HARRIET	But you can't show it.
MARILYN	I guess not.
HARRIET	Sometimes you just wanna scream but no sounds come out, like in a dream.
MARILYN	That's it. But on stage I can scream all I like.
HARRIET	Me, I don't scream no more. I just smash my fist against the wall. Boy does that hurt. *(laughing)* So, when did you become an actress?
MARILYN	In school we were putting on a play. I wanted to be Snow White. But the teacher said I had to be the witch or I wouldn't be in the play at all. So, I was the witch.
HARRIET	I bet you were a good witch...*(mimicking witch)* Heh, heh, heh..
MARILYN	Yes I was. I won the drama prize. And that's when I decided to be an actress.
HARRIET	You can't always choose the parts, uh? Like you wanted to marry Howard, but you ended up with Charles. And now, you're pretty screwed up, uh?
MARILYN	*(thoughtful)* I suppose I am, in a way. Nobody knows but you.
HARRIET	I used to be screwed up a lot. Lucky my Mom and Dad adopted me.
MARILYN	When was this?
HARRIET	I was six. They had kids of their own, all boys. Anyhow, they wanted a girl. *(laughing)* They thought I was nice and quiet. I sure fooled them. Fact is, I didn't even like them at first. *(rising)*
MARILYN	Why not?

HARRIET	Didn't trust nobody. People always burnin' and dumpin' you. I thought they'd be the same but they turned out real nice.

> MARILYN *is now sitting on the bench.* HARRIET *withdraws the shoelace she had taken from the garbage can and plays 'cat's cradle' as she speaks.*

HARRIET	My Mom and Dad never gave up on me. When I was in jail they always came and took me home, even when I screamed and told them to go away. When I was smashed and stoned, they never locked me out. Once I hit the teacher because she was mean. And beat up kids that called me stupid. You see, in school I always got the wrong answers. I got fed up so I quit. Anyhow I got no patience for learning...*(knotting the string as she speaks)* Mom and Dad took me to shrinks and social workers, but I wouldn't talk to nobody. You can't talk about feelings, 'specially when you're little, and you don't understand them. Would you've given up on me?
MARILYN	No.
HARRIET	*(throwing the knotted shoe lace at* MARILYN*'s feet)* Sure you would! I come from your belly and you gave me away before you even knew me. Why'd you do that? If I had a kid I'd keep her no matter what.
MARILYN	*(rising)* I told you I couldn't!
HARRIET	Bullshit! You're mean and selfish. You're not my mother! Mothers don't give their kids away. *(moving away from* MARILYN *toward the garbage can)*
MARILYN	*(pause)* I'm glad you have a good family.

HARRIET	*(picking up the teddy bear)* Yeah, I got my own room with a big tree outside the window and crazy squirrels runnin' up and down. And I got hundreds of tapes. Mom don't I care if my room's messy, so long's there's no bugs or cockroaches. There ain't none no more, since I don't bring in no more stray cats and frogs. All she cares about is the noise. I play my music real loud and it gives her a headache. When she plays her Frank Sinatra you can hear it in Hawaii.

MARILYN *toys with the shoelace.*

HARRIET	I suppose if you'd kept me I'd be someone else. Like polite and go to university. I wonder if I'd like being someone else. If I wasn't me, I wouldn't know what it's like to be me. And I like being me.
MARILYN	If you came with me, you could still be yourself.
HARRIET	You really want me, huh? Just like I am.
MARILYN	Yes.
HARRIET	But if you forced me to do things I don't want, I'd run away and be like those lost kids on milk cartons.
MARILYN	I wouldn't force you.
HARRIET	Mom and Dad used to fight a lot about me. When I came home at 4:00 in the morning, Mom yelled I shouldn't be out so late, I'll get killed on the street. Dad said I can take care'f myself, so long as I come home it's okay. *(picking up the skipping rope)* Mom wanted to punish me, and Dad got mad 'cause he don't believe in punishment, so Mom would cry, and I'd listen to them fight and think they're gonna break up.
MARILYN	I suppose they never did.

HARRIET	No. *(skipping rope slowly)* They always made up in the end, and I'd feel lousy and go lie on their bed. We'd hug and laugh a lot. I used to worry one' f them would die and I'd be sent away again. The next day I slept till four in the afternoon. Mom made me tea when I got up with a headache. *(laughing)* And I didn't have to go to school.
MARILYN	It would be nice to have a daughter. We could be friends.
HARRIET	You got no friends?
MARILYN	Not like you. We could really talk about things and share everything.
HARRIET	Like I could go with you to rehearsal and maybe be an actress someday? *(picking up the ball)*
MARILYN	Maybe.
HARRIET	I don't know if I could memorize all the lines.
MARILYN	I'd help you. *(rising from bench)*
HARRIET	And I could be famous, uh?
MARILYN	If you were good.
HARRIET	*(throwing ball to MARILYN)* What's it like in your house? What do you do all day?

> HARRIET *and* MARILYN *can toss the ball back and forth during following.*

MARILYN	In the morning I make breakfast for the boys.
HARRIET	Scrambled eggs and porridge?
MARILYN	Or pancakes.

HARRIET	My Mom makes the best porridge. It's lumpy and sticky but I like it that way. So what happens next?
MARILYN	After they go to school, I take exercise classes, and rehearse plays, read scripts.
HARRIET	What would I do?
MARILYN	You could play tennis with me.
HARRIET	You play good?
MARILYN	Pretty good.
HARRIET	Was Howard good in sports?
MARILYN	He played soccer.
HARRIET	So that's why I'm good in sports! I just don't like to play games much. You gotta show for practice and there's too many rules. I got kicked off the team for fighting. So what else do you do? You go on vacation?
MARILYN	Yes.
HARRIET	Me too. *(tossing ball back into garbage can and moving toward the wading pool where she toys with pebbles)* When Dad has to work, I go with Mom and my brother, Sam. To horse camp and New York to the zoo and science museums. You see bones of dead people and you imagine what they thought about. If they sweated in summer, what language they talked. If they hurt people. If I was smart in school I'd go for zoology.
MARILYN	You *are* smart.
HARRIET	*(tossing pebbles into pool)* What do you know about it? I told you I got no patience for learning.

MARILYN	If you studied something that interests you...
HARRIET	I ain't interested in nothing.
MARILYN	You were interested in finding me, and you did.
HARRIET	My Mom helped me. I couldn't do it alone.
MARILYN	I think you're a very capable girl.
HARRIET	*(rising from edge of pool)* Look, your boys can practice violin for a hundred hours. Me, I can't do that. You'd get mad at me.
MARILYN	I wouldn't. I'd be good to you. You wouldn't have to...
HARRIET	Wow! It's just like I told my Mom when she bugged me to do homework. I said: "You ain't my real mother. You can't tell me what to do. My real mother wouldn't force me to do nothin' I don't want." That used to make her so sad. She'd go off in a corner and cry, and I didn't even feel sorry. I don't do that no more.
MARILYN	All these years, I never forgot you. I really wanted you. You're my daughter. You belong with me. Please, come home with me.
HARRIET	You do want me.
MARILYN	Yes. With all my heart. There's always been something missing. It was you.
HARRIET	You were missing me? Like not knowing where I was and what I was doin'?
MARILYN	Yes.
HARRIET	That must've been awful for you.
MARILYN	We could start all over. The two of us.

HARRIET	But my Dad...He's got this garage and sometimes I work with him a couple'f hours. When we walk home I hold his big, rough hand. He smells good, from grease and gasoline. We have real good talks. About how he took an engine apart. About carburetors and fuel pumps. He tells me we have to be happy with what we got, 'cause there's lots of people worse off than us. Things like that.
MARILYN	Please, Harriet...*(reaching out for her)*
HARRIET	Look, I'm sick of talkin' to you. Why don't you go to your theatre and choke on the cord.
MARILYN	I'd rather stay with you.
HARRIET	You're gonna miss the play.
MARILYN	I have an understudy.
HARRIET	You're ready to give it up for me?
MARILYN	Yes.
HARRIET	Well, maybe you ain't so bad after all.
MARILYN	*(putting her arm around her)* I'd be so happy.

> HARRIET *moves away from her and sits on the bench.*

MARILYN	*(going to her)* What's the matter?

> MARILYN *goes to sit beside her.*

HARRIET	About a year ago I got so low, lyin' in the gutter, completely messed up. My Mom said I could only go up, 'cause I was as low as you can get. The only worse you can get is dead.

HARRIET   *(continued)* All'f a sudden I didn't wanna die. I mean stuck down in the earth, and never see my crazy squirrels, and the Moon-People or hear my music. Anyhow, I told my Mom I gotta know who my mother is. She looked so upset, I patted her on the bum and said *she* was my real mother. I only meant the woman who gave birth to me 'cause not knowin' was makin' me nervous. So she said she' d help me find you. She wrote a million letters, went to hospitals, and talked to the Agency people all over the place. It was like being a detective only much harder, 'cause no one wants to tell you nothin'. Anyhow, she found you so here I am. *(rising)* She wanted to come with me. She thought it'd be hard for me to do it alone. But I said I gotta do it myself. She gave me lots of money for the train ticket and the hotel -- we live about 600 miles away. She ain't scared I'll leave her and go to you. She says she only wants me to be happy. That's love, you know. When you don't care about yourself, just the other person.

MARILYN   She must be very special.

HARRIET   Ah, she ain't so special. She's got big ears she hides with her hair. She's a little fat and always goin' on a diet, then eats chocolate and gets fat again. She ain't so pretty, but she smiles with her eyes. My Dad's very handsome and strong. He cried a little when I left. He thought I didn't see 'cause at the station he turned his head around. My brother, Sam, came too. He's older but don't look it 'cause he's shorter than me. He's always buyin' me stuff like caps and belts. Yeah, they sure care about me. Must be my terrific personality.

MARILYN   Must be.

HARRIET   I'm gonna buy Mom a present, she likes flowers. I'll buy her roses, they're pretty and smell nice. Your kids ever buy you roses?

MARILYN	No.
HARRIET	I guess they don't love you enough.

MARILYN *tries to stifle her tears.*

HARRIET	Hey, don't cry, you want a rose, I'll buy you one. After all, if it wasn't for you I wouldn't be born.
MARILYN	Harriet, I want you to come home with me. Please.
HARRIET	It sure would be nice to be rich and go on vacation on them long love-boats. And visit Hollywood and ski in Switzerland. And have my own stereo and Harley Davidson. Maybe a black leather jacket and big goggles.
MARILYN	Yes.
HARRIET	Sounds good, just like a happy ending.
MARILYN	We'll have good times.
HARRIET	And maybe I'll have a couple of horses, like in those cowboy pictures. And invite rock stars to play at my parties. (*sitting on bench beside* MARILYN)
MARILYN	I'm not sure about rock stars.
HARRIET	But the horses, that's okay?
MARILYN	We have a place in Vermont. We'll get you a horse.
HARRIET	Wow! My Mom and Dad don't got no country place, and they can't get me a horse.
MARILYN	So what do you say?
HARRIET	It'd be just like with the Moon People. Only it'd be real.

MARILYN	Yes.
HARRIET	And what'll all your friends and relatives say when I show up? I'm supposed to be a big secret. They won't like you so much.
MARILYN	I always cared too much about what people will say. And not enough about what I want. I want you, Harriet, and nothing else matters. *(smiling, speaking like* HARRIET*)* And if they don't like it they can lump it.
HARRIET	*(pause)* Now that I'm not screwed up you want me, uh?
MARILYN	It's not like that...
HARRIET	Where were you when I was gettin' pushed around and lyin' in the gutter, uh?
MARILYN	I didn't know! That's not my fault!
HARRIET	Look here, Mrs. Perkyns, I don't care if you got a Snow-White castle and a swimming pool. I don't care if you got six color TVs and a Porche and a stable with twenty horses. That's not important. What's important is I got somethin' you can't never give me. So get the hell out of here, okay! Just go! *(throwing keys at her)*

MARILYN *is unable to move.*

HARRIET	Didn't you hear me? I told you to get lost.
MARILYN	I know you're hurt. I'm sorry. I do want to make it up to you. *(retrieving her keys)*
HARRIET	Okay, okay.

MARILYN *starts collecting her things.*

HARRIET	Comb your hair, you look like somethin' the cat dragged in.

> HARRIET *gives* MARILYN *her comb.*
> MARILYN *passes comb through her hair.*

MARILYN   Just for the record, there's no asthma in my family.

HARRIET   Good.

MARILYN   *(slipping on her shoes)* Are you going to look for your father?

HARRIET   I got a father. If you mean the guy who knocked you up, he's not worth me talkin' to him.

MARILYN   Sometimes we do things and don't think them through to the end. He may be sorry too. But like you said, once you say the wrong words, things don't turn out like they're supposed to. Also, for the record, he was very nice. Just scared, I suppose. Like me.

HARRIET   Well, I ain't scared no more.

MARILYN   I'm glad I met you.

HARRIET   Ah, you're not so bad. You could've turned out a lot worse.

MARILYN   You forgive me?

HARRIET   Yeah, sure, what the hell...

MARILYN   What will you do now?

HARRIET   First, I'm goin' back home, and tell my Mom and Dad I saw you. Then maybe I'll travel 'round the world a bit. Marry a good guy, a garage man like my Dad, and have a baby I'll take care of real good.

> HARRIET *picks up the teddy bear.*

HARRIET   Here take the teddy bear to be a souvenir from
                   me. He's from the garbage, but if you fix him up
                   he'll be real nice.

MARILYN   *(accepting the teddy bear)* May I have your
                   address?

                           HARRIET *fishes card out of her jacket
                           pocket, hands it to* MARILYN.

HARRIET   If you wanna get your car fixed sometime, here's
                   my Dad's card. He does a good job.

                           MARILYN *looks at the card, then drops
                           it into her bag.*

MARILYN   Thanks. I'll be in touch.

HARRIET   If we visit here sometime, we'll go see you in a
                   play. And I'll introduce you to my Mom. She
                   likes movies and actors.

MARILYN   Sure.

HARRIET   Hey, you better hurry. You can still be on time.
                   Have a good performance.

MARILYN   I'm glad you found me.

HARRIET   Yeah, sure. Sorry about gettin' you all wet.

MARILYN   I-pie d-pid l-pove y-poo.

                           MARILYN *takes one last look at*
                           HARRIET *and exits.*

HARRIET *(deciphering words)* I...did...love...you.

> *Music fades in.* HARRIET *takes* MARILYN's *bottle of perfume out of her pocket, smells it, returns the bottle to her pocket. The other items remain on and around the bench. She tosses a pebble into the water, and exits. Music continues for a moment along with some sounds from the playground, then fades out.*

> *The End.*

HURRAY FOR JOHNNY CANUCK

KEN GASS

Ken Gass was born in 1945 in Abbotsford, B.C., and attended the University of British Columbia theatre program before moving to Toronto in 1968. He founded the Factory Theatre in 1970 and remained artistic director of the company until 1979. This important company has premiered more than 100 new Canadian plays, including Gass' *Hurray for Johnny Canuck, The Boy Bishop,* and *Winter Offensive.* For much of the past ten years, Ken Gass has been working in radio, film, and television. His feature-length TV scripts include *Passion of the Patriots*, and the award-winning *The Squamish Five.* His current projects include two new stage plays, *Amazon Dream* and *Claudius*, as well as a film version of *Hurray for Johnny Canuck.*

AUTHOR'S INTRODUCTION

During World War II, the Canadian government placed an embargo on imported "non-essential reading material" such as magazines and comic books to help the Canadian balance of payments. As a result, a series of Canadian comic books sprang up to fill the gap. At first they imitated American models such as Captain America, but gradually their own style developed. For a time, a whole Canadian popular-art form flourished, but with the end of the war the embargo was lifted and Canadian comic books were squeezed out of the market.

The Canadian comics which this play reflects are an accurate mirror of Canadian attitudes during the war: the desire to overthrow the Nazi menace, the heroism of Canada's fighting men, as well as a tendency towards quick generalizations that are clearly racist by today's standards.

Hurray for Johnny Canuck evokes some of the nostalgia for old-fashioned heroism (who said Canada didn't have its own heroes?) but also enjoys sending up these values. The characters are affectionately satirized for their excesses. It may be an interesting exercise to look at some of the original comics to see how the characters have been changed for this play, and the way various episodes have been woven together to create one extended narrative. The style of the play, especially in the narration, borrows as well from the radio serials of the 1940's. However the play is clearly written from a contemporary viewpoint and the distance we have moved since the war years allows us to laugh at many of the attitudes of that earlier era.

Much of the joy of *Johnny Canuck* comes from creating a theatrical style that can exploit all mechanics of stage productions. If the play is produced in a proscenium arch theatre, a false proscenium should be built with the framework and prop cupboards and costume racks made a part of the set. Audiences enjoy seeing all the backstage tricks as long as no one apologizes for them. Indeed, here they can be satirized. It would be a mistake for young actors playing these roles to think that they can get away with being merely silly. Though much of the play is silly in the best sense of the word -- "shameless", in fact - the actors approach their roles with earnestness. Our heroes have clear objectives which they pursue against all odds, and often accomplish great deeds single-handedly. Of course, one can still acknowledge the audience, and play "out front", but it is important not to do all the audience's work for them. Most of the scenes are comic enough in terms of situation and character and do not need "mugging".

Research into the period is a great help for production, especially radio serials, newspapers, magazines and, of course, the comics themselves. Props and costumes need not be complex, as long as they are created with a sense of fun. The stage directions in the play can be simplified or expanded, depending on the production situation, as can casting requirements. Live accompaniment is a great asset if possible and simple conventions can be established for gunshots and other sound effects. Above all, everyone involved in the production -- cast, audience, and crew -- should have a good time.

Ken Gass

Hurray for Johnny Canuck was first produced at Factory Theatre Lab, Toronto, in November, 1974 with the following cast:

NARRATOR/MUSICIAN	*George Bassingthwaighte*
JOHNNY CANUCK	*Wally Michaels*
RUTH BARTON	*Patti Elsasser*
CORPORAL DIXON	*Jim Henshaw*
DEREK BRAS D'OR	*Maury Chaykin*
MAJOR DOMO	*Jank Zajfman*

Directed by Ken Gass.
Settings and visual contributions by Eric Steiner.
Music by George Bassingthwaighte.

Collaborators: *Hrant Alianak* and the original cast: *Maury Chaykin, Patti Elsasser, Jim Henshaw, Wally Michaels,* and *Jank Zajfman.*

Hurray for Johnny Canuck is based on Bell Comics of Canada (1941- 45) © Nelvana Ltd.

THE CHARACTERS

NARRATOR/MUSICIAN

JOHNNY CANUCK	Also plays Laddie and the Queen.
RUTH BARTON	Also plays Mom and Fraulein Fanny.
CORPORAL DIXON	Also plays Brian, Customs Officer, Otto, Goebbels, Guards, and Ricky von Schwinden.
DEREK BRAS D'OR	Also plays Pop, Bormann, Churchill, Guard, Black Hans, Captain America.
MAJOR DOMO	Also plays Checkers, Announcer, the King, Spy, Guard, Hitler, Schwarz.

THE SET

Preferably a mock proscenium with little footlights. Cartoon panels that change from scene to scene, a trap door, a gaudy curtain, a props and costume cupboard on each side of the stage. All the mechanics of the performance should be visible and done with as much fun and mischief as possible.

PROLOGUE

NARRATOR   Ladies and Gentlemen, our National Anthem.

> *The Anthem, "0 Canada", is played.*
> *Cast sings it raucously. There is a*
> *"Hurray for Johnny Canuck" sign above*
> *the proscenium arch with flashing lights*
> *that come on with the following.*

NARRATOR   What you are about to witness is an absolutely
factual, historical document of how Johnny
Canuck and the secret Canadian Supersquad saved
the world from the evil, sneaky, dirty, fascist,
Nazi, anti-democratic menace of men like
Hirohito, Mussolini, and Adolf Hitler, as
authenticated by Bell Comics of Canada.

***

Sc. i. -- AROUND THE RADIO

> *All props are two-dimensional cut-outs.*
> *The radio is a cardboard cut-out.* MOM
> *is dusting.* BRIAN *is reading his*
> *comics.* POP *sits staring vacantly.*

NARRATOR   In the quiet of Canadian villages like this one,
the family huddle around the radio, waiting for
words that could change their destiny. It is early
August; the year, 1939.

BRIAN   Hey, Pop! This Captain Marvel is really great. I
wish I could do things like that.

POP   Well, maybe you'll get a chance to do that very
thing once that war they're talking about in
Europe gets started.

BRIAN   Gee, Pop, do you really think so?

MOM	Be quiet, Brian. It's time for the news.
ANNOUNCER	Here are the six o'clock news headlines. In London, Prime Minister Neville Chamberlain *(as MOM sharply turns up volume)* happily announced to a cheering crowd that he is convinced that Germany poses no threat to European security or world peace. In Berlin, Adolf Hitler reaffirmed his pledge to respect European borders and live in peace with Britain. Officials in Ottawa today stated that these actions make the prospect of war unlikely. In southern Saskatchewan, rapeseed farmers again complained...
MOM	*(turning off radio)* Well, thank goodness for that. So you boys can just fix your thoughts on harvesting that wheat and never mind all this foolish thought about going off to war.
BRIAN	Ah, gee! Maw!
MOM	And never you mind those comics, your chores are waiting.
BRIAN	I never get to have any fun. *(exiting)*
MOM	And you, you're just as bad...
POP	The boy's just craving a little excitement is all, fer cripes sake.
MOM	Well, who isn't? *(exiting)*

***

Sc. ii. -- DANGER IN THE NORTH -- *Part One*

> *The curtain opens on* DIXON *and* LADDIE *in a frozen tableau. A props girl throws cardboard snow over them. The background is northern wilderness and a lonely cabin.*

NARRATOR   But far in the most northern reaches of Canada,
                Corporal Dixon, tireless officer of the Royal
                Canadian Mounted Police, was hot on the trail of
                another evil menace. The story thus far:
                Following a complaint by a friendly Indian chief
                that some of his tribe were receiving deadly
                drugs, Corporal Dixon and his faithful
                companion, Laddie, pursue the drug's source.
                Advice from a dying loyal Eskimo has lead them
                to the trail of a mad trapper called Checkers.

DIXON   *(after fighting through the raging blizzard)* Whoa,
                there, Laddie, good dog. I think we'd better wait
                here for a moment until this blizzard blows over.
                Blazes, I hope it doesn't last too long; we sure
                don't want to lose Checkers' trail, do we?

                LADDIE *barks agreeably.*

DIXON   Right now, it seems that only a few Indians have
                been exposed to the drug menace, but, who
                knows, before long, it could reach the white
                settlements as well. Good boy, Laddie, just rest
                easy. Why don't we share one of these chocolate
                cookies? Mmmm, good. Keeps the cold out.
                *(singing a few bars from "Rosemarie", very poor
                Nelson Eddy imitation with* LADDIE *joining in
                on the last line)* Come on, Laddie, we'd better get
                moving before we lose the trail. Just a bit
                further.

                LADDIE *moves away and barks
                sharply.*

DIXON   What's the matter? Blazes, this isn't like you,
                Laddie. Mush! Forward. *(prodding* LADDIE *who
                is still protesting)* Now, straighten out! Come
                on, Laddie, follow me.

                DIXON *goes forward and* LADDIE
                *grabs his ankle cuff just as he falls into
                a deep chasm.* LADDIE *pulls him out.*

DIXON	Blazes, what is this?
LADDIE	*(his thoughts, on a comic book caption)* "You fool, Dixon!"
DIXON	A deep chasm, I nearly fell into it. By tar, you saved my life, Laddie. Good boy!
LADDIE	*(thoughts)* "Never mind the compliments, just give me a chocolate."
DIXON	Good boy, Laddie. Here, have a chocolate cookie. *(as electric organ war-dance music creeps in)* Blazes, look into that chasm, Laddie. It's...why, it's a girl, I think she's being held captive, and look! Those people, crazy dancing Indians and, look! Could it be, why, I think it is...Nazis! What could Nazis be doing in the north? Laddie, we've got to find a way down into that chasm, look for a path. *(lifting up a trap door)* Look! a crevice in the rock. Come on, good fella, I just hope we're not too late. *(disappearing together into trap door)*
NARRATOR	Will Corporal Dixon and his faithful companion, Laddie, reach the mysterious girl in time to save her from torture? Watch as we return to the adventures of Dixon in the frozen north.

Curtains close.

***

DANGER IN THE NORTH -- *Part Two*

> NARRATOR *stretches, then the curtains open.*

NARRATOR	Back with Corporal Dixon and his faithful companion, Laddie. The story thus far. Rescued from a close brush with death down an icy chasm by Laddie, the daring duo witness a gruesome scene below.

> RUTH BARTON *walks on, strapped to a large, two-dimensional rock. A weird trapper called* CHECKERS, *wearing a strange mask and a devil's fork, dances around like a madman.*

RUTH   It doesn't matter what you do to me, I won't betray my Eskimo friends.

CHECKERS   Aaaaaaaaaaaahhhhh! *(dancing off)*

> *During the next narration,* DIXON *and* LADDIE *carry in a mountain then peer over the top of it.*

NARRATOR   Trapped in the slow descent down the icy cliffs, Dixon and Laddie observe the scene helplessly from a distance.

DIXON   We must hurry, Laddie. That girl is in dire danger. If only there was some way to get there more quickly. Blazes, Laddie! Be careful.

> LADDIE *falls into the back gutter with a long howl.*

DIXON   He's gone. Poor fellow. Such a good dog is hard to find. Wait! By tar, he's landed on a ledge. *(as* LADDIE's *paw appears)* He's moving. He's all right. I can't wait any longer. I've got to take the chance. *(with a shout, leaping into the chasm)*

> BORMANN *enters from another entrance, pulling* CHECKERS *by the ear.*

BORMANN   Excuses, excuses. You expect me to take excuses back to der Fuhrer? Vhy can't you make dis fool voman cooperate?

CHECKERS   She's no ordinary woman. She works for the Canadian Red Cross.

BORMANN   Let me talk to her. *(closing on her)* Listen, my dear, ve are goot people. Ve are not going to hurt you. Ve are going to build a master race to help mankind, but you must tell your Eskimo people to transport our supplies.

RUTH   Do you think I'm a fool? I know an evil face when I see one.

BORMANN   OOOOH! Vot stubborness. Vot idiotness. Vot... Vot am I going to tell der Fuhrer? My dear, you are very pretty. Kiss me. *(as* RUTH *spits in his face)* Kill her! Ve must tink of something else.

> *As* BORMANN *exits,* CHECKERS *leaps with a scream of delight and rushes to the prop cupboard, bringing out some painted sticks and flames. He puts them under her legs and blows on the flames. With a final giddy scream, he dances out.*

RUTH   I guess this is the end.

> LADDIE *enters from a distance.*

RUTH   Wait! Is that a dog? *(as* LADDIE *stretches his leg in a formal pose)* It looks like a dog! It is a dog! It looks like Laddie! It is Laddie! Oh, thank heavens. That means Corporal Dixon has found me. Hurry, Laddie. Cut through these ropes before these monsters return.

> LADDIE *is tugging at her dress. Enter* CHECKERS.

CHECKERS   What is this? A dog?

> CHECKERS *and* LADDIE *growl at each other.* CHECKERS *lunges with his fork and misses.* LADDIE *goes for his throat and wrestles him dawn. Enter* BORMANN.

BORMANN   Vot iss das? Ein hund? *(aiming his pistol))*

>   DIXON *enters.*

DIXON   Hold it, Nazi!

>   DIXON *and* BORMANN *exchange fire.*
>   DIXON *is wounded.* BORMANN
>   *escapes.*

DIXON   My arm!

RUTH   Dixon!

DIXON   It's only a shoulder wound. Why, it's Ruth
Barton! What are you doing here?

RUTH   Untie me and I'll tell you.

DIXON   Of course. *(kicking flames down as* LADDIE
punches out CHECKERS*)* Good work, Laddie.
Go find the other one.

>   LADDIE *exits.* DIXON *unties one arm
>   and* RUTH *reveals a purse around her
>   wrist.*

RUTH   I'm sure glad you came when you did. Look out!

>   CHECKERS *has gotten up and charges*
>   DIXON *who turns just in time and
>   gives him a glancing blow which sends*
>   CHECKERS *to the edge of the cliff ,
>   where he loses his balance and falls with
>   a scream.* DIXON *is unable to save
>   him.*

DIXON   Poor fellow. Those rocks below are hard, too.

>   LADDIE *returns, barking. There is a
>   sound of an airplane.*

DIXON   What's that?

BORMANN   *(as he flies by in a two-dimensional airplane)* You cursed Canadians vill not get avay mit dis. Ve Chermans vill return! *(exiting, with* LADDIE *chasing him)*

DIXON   Tell me about your capture.

RUTH   Well, I was flying medical supplies to an Eskimo village near the Arctic Circle when our plane was forced down in bad weather. Seeking help, I was captured by this madman who tried to force me to distribute deadly drugs among the Indian and Eskimo villages.

DIXON   By tar, I believe that's the very drug ring that we were sent to break up!

LADDIE *barks.*

RUTH   Well, I'd better get back to my mission. Our medical supplies are very much needed in these parts.

DIXON   Are you sure you wouldn't like to come back to Ottawa with me?

RUTH   *(as* LADDIE *growls)* Not now, Corporal Dixon. But I'm sure we'll meet again soon on another adventure. Good-bye. And thank you again, Corporal Dixon. And thank you, Laddie. Good-bye. *(giving a delicate wave and disappearing)*

DIXON   Well, Laddie, at least we've destroyed the Deadly Drug Menace and kept those Nazis out of Canada. Let's go, Laddie. *(as they start off fighting the blizzard,* DIXON *stops)* She didn't even mention my wound.

***

Sc. iii. -- BUCKINGHAM PALACE HONOURS

> *The opening tableau includes palace windows looking out on St. James's Park, and two gaudy chairs. There is a guard with a tall busby. DIXON stands erect, brushing lint off his jacket.*

NARRATOR   In Buckingham Palace, Corporal Dixon receives a medal from King George VI for having kept the Nazi Menace out of the Canadian Colony.

> *As "God Save The King" is played, the KING and QUEEN enter waving. They are riding on a little red wagon which is being pulled through the gutter on a string. DIXON rises from his bow after a nudge from the GUARD. He shakes hands with the KING and also shakes the hand of the QUEEN, which he was supposed to kiss.*

KING   At ease, Corporal Dixon.

> *DIXON smiles, but can't say anything. The QUEEN smiles. She begins to cross her knees, then pushes her knee down.*

KING   *(beginning his public speech)* During troubled times like these, it warms the heart of Mother England to know that her Colonial Children will unite to support her in her struggle against Imperialism, I mean, Fascism.

> *The QUEEN coughs.*

KING   We have here an example of classic Canadian courage. Corporal Dixon, with men like you -- like you --

QUEEN   Mother England knows --

KING	Mother England knows that she, that she --
QUEEN	Can win the victory --
KING	That she can win the victory against the Nazi menace that threatens all the democracies of the world.
QUEEN	Wrap it up now.
KING	And so that you, Corporal Dixon, may encourage Canadians all over that Dominion to follow your example of courage, bravery and heroism, we place this medal...

> DIXON *is nudged forward and the velcro medal is pounded on his chest.*

KING	...for all to see.

> DIXON *shakes the* KING's *hand awkwardly, bows to the* QUEEN *and shakes her extended hand as well. She grimaces then rises and speaks to audience.*

QUEEN	The lovely people of Canada, her glorious rivers, mountains and scenery, her brave sailors, soldiers and airmen. We shall always love! *(as she exits, to the* KING*)* Come along.

> *They exit to a great swelling of music, riding their red wagon, as* DIXON *rubs his medal with great pride.*

***

Sc. iv. -- THE HEROES WITH MOTHER NATURE

> *The woods of northern Ontario. Three*
> *large cut-out trees are on stage, as well*
> *as a stump and scenic background.*
> *JOHN CAMPELL and DEREK*
> *DUFOIS are chopping down trees with*
> *large two-dimensional axes. DEREK is*
> *singing, JOHNNY is whistling, and*
> *there are all kinds of birds and other*
> *'critters' making sounds offstage.*

NARRATOR The war fever escalates, as all of Europe is turned into a boiling inferno of actions! Thrills and adventures! On the home-front, Canadians are not idle. At this very moment Mackenzie King, the memorable Prime Minister, has sent Corporal Dixon on an assignment to recruit a Canadian superfighter.

JOHN *(after some exercise)* Ah, there's nothing like the Canadian Shield to put muscles on your back and red blood in your veins, right, Derek?

DEREK Waneau, regarde, jolie waneau.

JOHN Oh yes, pretty critters, those birds. Okay, Derek, do you think we can finish off this mountainside before suppertime?

DEREK Waneau! Waneau!

JOHN Later, Derek, later. Now, you swing to the left and I'll swing to the right and we won't stop till we reach the top of the mountain, okay?

DEREK Waneau!

JOHN Never mind. When we get to the top, we can have a chocolate bar.

DEREK Chocolat! Chocolat!

> DEREK *starts swinging his axe with incredible speed.* DIXON *enters the scene to a fine phrase of music.*

DIXON　　Hey, guys! Hey, can you guys slow down a minute? Hey, guys!

JOHN　　Hey, look out, there's a tree coming down your way. *(diving on* DIXON, *knocking him aside as the tree falls down)*

Are you all right, sonny?

DIXON　　Yes. I just seem to have this tree on my leg.

JOHN　　Mmm, let me see...I can't...Derek, can you move this tree? Derek!

DEREK　　*(who is still chopping away)* Vite, vite, Johnny, chocolat.

JOHN　　Never mind. Move the tree.

DEREK　　Qu'est-ce que c'est? Tree? *(laughing, then lifting tree up with two fingers)*

DIXON　　Blazes, you wouldn't be Johnny Canuck, by any chance, would you?

JOHN　　'Fraid not, my name's John Campell. And this is Derek Dufois.

DIXON　　I'm Corporal Dixon. Pleased to meet you.

> *They shake hands. Then* DEREK *refuses to let go of* DIXON's *hand until* JOHN *offers him a chocolate.* DIXON *hops away like a rabbit, nursing his hand.*

JOHN　　How'd you like to join us for coffee, Dixon? *(his coffee pot is stuck to his two-dimensional lunch bucket)*

DIXON	Great. You sure you never heard of Johnny Canuck?
JOHN	Nope. Derek, you heard of Johnny Canuck?
DEREK	Waneau. Regarde, waneau.
DIXON	What'd he say?
JOHN	Just talking to his friends.
DIXON	Say, where are the rest of the lumberjacks?
JOHN	Just us here.
DIXON	You mean you're clearing this whole mountain by yourselves?
JOHN	Just me and Derek.
DIXON	Well, by tar and blazes, you're the man I want!
JOHN	What's that? I've never broken the law in my life.
DIXON	Mr. Campbell, how'd you like to become Johnny Canuck?
JOHN	That's a silly name.
DIXON	Johnny Canuck is the symbol of free Canada. Canada needs Johnny Canuck to build its image as a freedom-loving Nazi-hating country. In short, we need you to lead the Canadian war effort. We need you to destroy the Bosch.
DEREK	*(seizing up)* Bosch? Bosch? *(going on a rampage, knocking down trees)*
JOHN	No, Derek, no, no Bosch. Waneau. Waneau. Waneau!
DEREK	Waneau. Ou est waneau?

JOHN   Waneau. *(aside to* DIXON*)* He hates the Bosch.

DIXON   I want to see that again. Derek.

JOHN   I wouldn't if I were you, mister.

DIXON   Relax. I'm a police officer, John. Derek. Derek. Come here. Bosch.

DEREK   Bosch? Bosch?

> DEREK *goes berserk and lifts* DIXON *off the ground by the neck and lays him down, strangling him.*

JOHN   I warned you. Derek. Waneau. Waneau, Derek. Waneau! *(the strangling continues unabated)* This calls for drastic action. *(running to stump)* Derek, patate frite. Patate frite.

DEREK   Patate frite! *(grabbing the French fries and calming down like a baby with his food)*

DIXON   Gentlemen. *(his voice is very high)* Gentlemen -- *(voice medium)* Gentlemen -- *(voice at its usual low register)* I have the honour of recruiting you into the secret Canadian supersquad. You will report to Mackenzie King immediately and receive your first European assignment.

JOHN   Europe, gee, that's good of you, but Derek and I couldn't leave Canada.

DIXON   Why not?

JOHN   Well, you see, we love this land, these rugged mountains, these giant trees, these sparkling lakes, this epic of nature...

DIXON   Then you must do your duty to protect this land from the Evil Menace that threatens the entire world. The dirty Bosch --

DEREK	Bosch!
DIXON	Patate frite, patate frite!
DEREK	Patate frite.
DIXON	The, uh, evil menace is almost upon us. Only you can save Canada.
JOHN	Well, when you put it that way, I guess we have no choice. When do we start?
DIXON	You start now. Maestro, can you give us a chord?

> *Music. He holds out a* JOHNNY CANUCK *sweat shirt.*

DIXON	Your name is Johnny Canuck. And, you, Derek, friend, what can we call you? Arms of steel, arms of gold, how do you say "golden arms" in French?
JOHN	Er, er, Bras, and Or, Bras d'Or.
DIXON	The birth of Johnny Canuck and Derek Bras d'Or! Freedom fighters of Canada.

> *JOHNNY is posed next to DEREK as the "Hurray" lights flash. DEREK continues trying to find the last French fry in the box.*

***

Sc. v. -- NEWS OF TERROR

> *The scene is similar to Scene One; the family again huddles around the radio.*

NARRATOR	In May, 1940, the family again huddles around the radio to hear a fearful broadcast.

The radio makes its newscast beeps.

MOM Oh, do we have to listen to those horror stories
again?

POP Well, how else is a fella gonna find out what's
going on in the world fer cripes sakes?

ANNOUNCER Here are the six o'clock news headlines: Today,
thousands of German bombers and more than ten
thousand land troops made a coordinated assault
on Holland, Belgium and defenseless
Luxembourg. All three countries have nearly
crumbled under the weight of the Nazi blitzkrieg.
Winston Churchill, in his opening address as
Prime Minister of England, appealed to all of
England's colonies to make the cause of freedom
their own.

BRIAN That does it, Maw! I'm going off to fight the
dirty Huns.

MOM Now wait a minute, Brian. You're not Johnny
Canuck, you know. It's real bombs and bullets
that you'll be dealing with.

BRIAN It's too late, Maw. I enlisted this morning.

MOM You didn't!

POP Is that true, son? *(as* BRIAN *nods)* Well, how
about that!

MOM Paw! You've got to stop the boy!

POP The boy's a man now, Mother.

BRIAN Sorry, Maw. I'm on my way. *(exiting)*

MOM *(after him)* Well, make sure you keep warm
and...make sure you write your maw and paw. I
don't want to sit here waiting for one of those
telegrams to find out what happened.

Sc. vi. -- THE SECRET FRANKFURT LANDING

	The scene is the Frankfurt airport. The panels show barbed wire, planes in the distance and the dreaded swastika. As the curtain opens, a small wooden plane flies down a string to make a landing.
NARRATOR	Johnny Canuck and Derek Bras d'Or, heroes of the Canadian Supersquad, arrive in Germany to sabotage Hitler's war machine. The daring duo arrive at the Frankfurt airport, disguised as Austrian tourists.
	JOHNNY and DEREK emerge in tourist garb: short pants, odd hats and cameras. They carry two-dimensional suitcases.
DEREK	Au revoir, waneau. Au revoir, waneau. Johnny, c'est le grand waneau.
JOHNNY	Yes, Derek, but we mustn't look suspicious. These Bosch mustn't suspect that we're Canadians.
DEREK	Bosch!
JOHNNY	Ssshhh. Someone's coming. Smile, Derek.
	JOHNNY takes his picture. They move to one side as RUTH comes in wearing a stewardess dress. She moves to one corner, looks around, then begins taking off her outfit .
JOHNNY	Good grief, Derek, what's that girl doing? No, don't look.
RUTH	Oh, oh. I've been spotted. I'll explain later. *(exiting into costume cupboard)*
JOHNNY	This is a very strange place, Derek. Maybe we'd better just get out of here.

DEREK   Oui, Johnny.

JOHNNY   Gee, I wish I knew my way around here.

                              SPY *enters with hot dogs.*

JOHNNY   Over here, Derek.

DEREK   *(sniffing as* SPY *passes.)* Hot dog, Johnny. Hot
               dog. Ou il y a hot dog, il y a aussi de patate frite.
               Patate frite.

JOHNNY   No, Derek. The Jerries don't eat patate frite, only
               hot dogs and sauerkraut.

DEREK   Pas de patate frite?

JOHNNY   No, Derek.

DEREK   Maudit Bosch.

                              Enter CUSTOMS OFFICER.

CUSTOMS   Are you gentlemen waiting to clear customs?

JOHNNY   Oh yes, er, Jawohl. *(gettng their bags and lining
               up)*

CUSTOMS   *(twirling pistol)* Do you haf anything to declare?

JOHNNY   No. Er, only our love for Chermany.

DEREK   Bosch!

JOHNNY   Waneau!

                              SPY *has returned with newspaper. He
                              observes the scene.* RUTH *has emerged
                              and watches the* SPY.

CUSTOMS   Vot ist? You are not German!

JOHNNY   Shucks, I was hoping to keep that our little
                secret, heinie.

                JOHNNY *suddenly KO's the*
                CUSTOMS OFFICER. *The* SPY *has*
                advanced and pulls out a pistol from
                behind.

RUTH   Look out!

                DEREK *turns around and by accident*
                sends the SPY *sprawling across the*
                stage.

DEREK   Oh, pardon, monsieur...

                JOHNNY *sees* RUTH *and tries to put*
                the CUSTOMS OFFICER *back in his*
                chair. JOHNNY*whistles.*

RUTH   *(after mysteriously crossing the stage)* Good
                work, Johnny. Good work, Derek.

JOHNNY   How do you know our names?

RUTH   I'm part of the Squad, Johnny. My name is Ruth
                Barton.

JOHNNY   Gee, Dixon didn't say anything about girls on
                this mission.

DEREK   Ruth Barton. *(waving shyly)*

RUTH   We suspected the Jerries would be laying a trap
                for you, so I came along in a different disguise.
                I've got a map that will lead us to the Resistance
                Headquarters in Berlin.

JOHNNY   Gosh, this is a very dangerous place for a girl.

RUTH   I'm not just any girl, Johnny. I'm Ruth Barton.
                Follow me.

DEREK   *(as they exit)* Johnny, Ruth Barton est tres jolie.

JOHNNY   Never mind, come on Derek.

> RUTH *smiles.* DEREK *lifts the*
> CUSTOMS OFFICER *from the floor*
> *with a light gesture as they exit.*

***

Sc. vii. TRAGEDY IN THE GERMAN UNDERGROUND

> *Headquarters of the German*
> *underground, Sign of Freedom. A*
> *basement room.* OTTO VON
> BERGNER *is speaking into a*
> *homemade radio.*

NARRATOR   Otto von Bergner, fearless young leader of the
               German Resistance Movement, is sending a
               clandestine message under the name Sign of
               Freedom to the people of Germany.

OTTO   This is the Sign of Freedom broadcasting to the
               people of Germany. People of Germany,
               remember the days when our country was at
               peace with the world, when the rest of Europe
               was our friend. Today, the German people are
               being forced to wage an inhuman war against our
               brothers. People of Germany, resist. When the
               Allied bombers bring ruination to your country
               and your loved ones, remember, you have only
               your Fuhrer to thank.

> A GUARD *with eyepatch and two-*
> *dimensional machine gun, has overheard*
> *the conversation and entered the room.*

GUARD   Schvein! You dare to betray der Vaterland! Gif
               me dat radio.

OTTO   No! This is the Sign of Freedom going off the
               air!

GUARD *pulls out wire and, as* OTTO
attacks, knocks him down.

GUARD   Little rat! You vill make no more broadcasts.
(shooting OTTO*)* In der name of der Fuhrer, die!
(exiting, smashing the radio on his way out)

NARRATOR   As Ruth Barton nears the Underground hideout,
she hears the shot. Her heart filled with fear, she
leads Johnny Canuck and Derek Bras d'Or to the
scene of Otto's slaughter.

They run in.

RUTH   Look, it must be Otto.

OTTO   Yes, my name was Otto. Who are you?

RUTH   My name is Ruth Barton. My friends and I are
from Canada. This is Derek Bras d'Or and this is
Johnny Canuck.

OTTO   Johnny Canuck! Johnny Canuck at last you have
come. But you have come in time only to see the
Sign of Freedom at its lowest hour. *(coughing)*
You brave Canadians must take my place.

JOHNNY   We will, Otto. Well destroy the Evil Menace
before it kills any more innocent people.

OTTO   Bless you, Johnny Canuck. The Sign of Freedom
lives on.

OTTO *dies.*

RUTH   *(lifting his hand up and then dropping it)* He's
dead, Johnny, he's dead.

DEREK   Il est mort? *(crying)*

JOHNNY   Be brave, Derek. Let's just be certain that he
didn't die in vain.

RUTH Yes, no time for tears. The entire German Underground is in danger. We must get a signal through to warn them to regroup. Let's see if the radio can be fixed.

> DEREK *carries* OTTO's *body out the back.*

JOHNNY Okay Ruth, I'll keep watch outside.

> JOHNNY *exits as* RUTH *twists and turns the radio antennae.*

NARRATOR Working feverishly against the ever present threat of Nazi patrols, Ruth struggles to repair the radio, the only source of contact among their German friends. Suddenly, Johnny races into the room.

> JOHNNY *and* DEREK *rush in from different sides.*

JOHNNY We must hurry. There's a whole squadron of Jerries on their way here.

RUTH I'm not leaving until I get this broadcast through. Our friends are in danger.

JOHNNY Okay, how long will you be?

RUTH A few minutes.

JOHNNY Okay, Derek, I guess this will be the first real test of Canadian strength. Are you ready for the Bosch? Derek?

DEREK Bosch! Bosch! *(starting on a rampage)*

JOHNNY Not yet, Derek.

RUTH Ah, I'm beginning to get a signal.

> GUARD *rushes in with machine gun.*

GUARD	Look. Dese underground schvein nefer stop. I vill haf to kill you all!
JOHNNY	Easier said than done, heinie.

> JOHNNY *dives low and tackles the GUARD, spinning him around then givng him a punch which sends him offstage.*

JOHNNY	Ah, nothing like a good game of rugby to keep you in shape. *(rushing offstage to check an entrance)*
RUTH	Sign of Freedom to German Underground. Nazi spies have penetrated location of secret cells. Abandon lodgings and regroup. Repeat, abandon lodgings and regroup. P.S. Do not despair; Johnny Canuck is here. This is the Sign of Freedom Broadcast.
GUARDS	*(rushing in)* Aha!
DEREK	Bosch, Bosch! *(grabbing them by the collars, spinning them around, then banging their heads together)*
JOHNNY	*(re-entering)* Good work, Derek.
DEREK	*(jumping up and down with glee)* Ils auront beaucoup de mal au tete!

> *Another* NAZI *runs in pointing a Luger.*

NAZI	You vill die now, Johnny Canuck, for dis insult to der Fuhrer.
RUTH	Not if I can help it, meathead!

> RUTH *kicks the pistol into the air, then grabs the* NAZI's *arm and flips him over. He lands heavily on the floor. The "Hurray for Johnny" lights come on.*

JOHNNY	Yes, I think we have already begun to avenge Otto's death. The Sign of Freedom and the German Underground, with our help, will survive! Ruth, you were wonderful!
RUTH	Not now, Johnny. Let's just go. *(they run out)*
DEREK	Chocolat! Chocolat, Johnny!

***

Sc. viii. -- IN THE OFFICE OF THE ARCH-FIEND

NARRATOR	Back in the chancellory, Adolf Hitler is preparing to expand the German invasion of Europe.
	The curtain opens to reveal HITLER *reading a Superman comic. His desk is very narrow. On it hangs a globe with darts in various countries. There is a knock on the door.*
HITLER	Password.
GOEBBELS	I forget, mein Fuhrer!
HITLER	Come in, Gobbles.
GOEBBELS	*(entering and tripping over his own feet)* I fell over, mein Fuhrer. *(getting up)* Gut morgen mein Fuhrer. You're going to be very proud of me dis morgen.
HITLER	I hope so. You haf der var report?
GOEBBELS	Every t'ing is progressing as planned, mein Fuhrer. Der occupation of France iss almost complete. Nein resistance. *(on each "resistance" he elbows* HITLER*)* Ve haf taken ofer der Netherlands, nein resistance. Finland, Luxembourg, Belgium, nein resistance, nein resistance, nein resistance.

HITLER   And vot about Deutschland?

GOEBBELS   Ver, mein Fuhrer?

HITLER   Deutschland, Deutschland!

GOEBBELS   Ahh, Deutschland, Deutschland, ein volk, ein reich, ein Fuhrer!

HITLER   Ein resistance?

GOEBBELS   Ein little resistance. It's dat Canuck fellow --

HITLER   Zo! Gobbles. Dumbkopf. Noodlehead. Pinball machine. Ver iss dat Canuck?

GOEBBELS   Mein Fuhrer, dat Canuck iss ein dead duck. *(pleased with phrase)* Ve are laying a trap for him, a trap from vich no one can hescape!

HITLER   You are an idiot. Everyday you promise me you vill arrest him, and everyday dat Canuck goes on destroying my var machine. Der Canadians are nothing. They are an inferior people and they know it. We are Germans, nein, nein?

GOEBBELS   Nein! I mean --

HITLER   Zo! Vhy can't you kill dose Canucks or torture dem or shoot dem in der back or strangle dem or beat dem up or something?

GOEBBELS   I don't know, mein Fuhrer.

HITLER   Everyday dat goes by mit out his capture, I think dat Canuck vill come here and kill me and den you vould become der Fuhrer and den vat vould happen to my master race?

GOEBBELS   Vell, mein Fuhrer, if I vas der --

HITLER   Silence! Answer der phone, Gobbles.

> *The phone then rings.* GOEBBELS *is confused.*

GOEBBELS   Gobbles, here, I mean, Goobles, Goebbles here. Vat? Vat? Vat? VAT? Vat, vat, vat?

> HITLER *wants the phone.* GOEBBELS *lifts up the whole desk and moves it away.*

GOEBBELS   Vat? Vat? Vat? Mein Fuhrer, you're going to be very proud of me, mein Fuhrer. Ve haf sighted Johnny Canuck and all his friends.

HITLER   Goot! Ver?

GOEBBELS   *(at phone)* Goot! Ver? *(to* HITLER*)* Inside der Berlin Munitions Plant! *(suddenly realizing why* HITLER *is not smiling)* Ach der liebe.

HITLER   Den vhy are you standing here? Go and get dem and don't come back mit out dem!

GOEBBELS   I'm going to get dem, mein Fuhrer, and I von't be back mit out dem! *(tripping)* I fell over again. *(exiting slowly)*

HITLER   Vot fools! *(at the phone)* Hello. You are fired! *(shooting his pistol into the phone)*

***

Sc. ix. -- THE MUNITIONS PLANT ESCAPADE

> *Two stagehands carry in a book flat representing a forbidding stone factory. A door is painted on part of one side of the flat.* JOHNNY, RUTH *and* DEREK *enter and place themselves outside the walls.*

NARRATOR	The story thus far. Having successfully restored the German Underground, Johnny Canuck, Derek Bras d'Or, and Ruth Barton are now planning their most daring mission of all: the destruction of Hitler's War Munitions Factory.
RUTH	No luck, Johnny. Nothing but concrete walls and *(knocking)* iron doors around here. The only way we're going to penetrate this fortress is through the skylights.
DEREK	Waneau, Johnny, waneau.
JOHNNY	You're right, Derek, can you give me a boost so I can reach the corner post.
DEREK	Jawohl. *(laughing as* RUTH *and* JOHNNY *are dumb-founded)* Un petit joke. *(lifting* JOHNNY *by the foot and with a grunt, hurling him into the air)*
RUTH	Oh, be careful, Johnny. We can't afford to lose you.
JOHNNY	Don't worry, Ruth. I won't be long.
NARRATOR	As Johnny attempts to scale the munitions fortress, Ruth and Derek wait anxiously for what seems an eternity. Suddenly, Ruth is startled by an approaching deadly shadow.
RUTH	Derek! Shhhh! It's a guard.
	DEREK *hides by a corner. The* GUARD *advances, doing an exaggerated goose-step. He passes* DEREK *who reaches out, grabbing him by the neck and strangling him easily.*
DEREK	Bosch!
RUTH	Good work, Derek. Listen, another one is coming.

> *This time it's from the opposite direction, so they hide in a different corner.*

GUARD Achtung!

> *GUARD cautiously steps towards the gate. After three steps, another GUARD appears at the other end.*

2ND GUARD Achtung!

RUTH Two of them?

> *The GUARDS move in unison, closer and closer to our heroes. RUTH crosses both fingers. Just as the GUARDS are ready to pounce, the rusty iron door opens and JOHNNY pulls RUTH and DEREK inside before closing the door. The GUARDS attack to find only each other.*

2ND GUARD Wolf?

1ST GUARD Ja, Kurt.

2ND GUARD *(speaking very poor German)* Wie kommts dese Canucks sich vexsheben konnten?

1ST GUARD *(speaking fluently)* Ich weiss nicht.

2ND GUARD Wir mussen nieman das ertzollen, weil der Fuhrer uns sheissen --

1ST GUARD Shiessen!

2ND GUARD Shiessen wirt, nichtwahr?

1ST GUARD Jawohl. Cigarette? Amerikanisher.

2ND GUARD Danke. Ich habe ein Englanshen feuer.

1ST GUARD	Danke. Eh, schmeckt!
2ND GUARD	Wolf?
1ST GUARD	Ja, Kurt?
2ND GUARD	Wie gehts deiner schoene Frau?
1ST GUARD	Ah nicht gut; sie ist etwas krank.
2ND GUARD	Ja?
1ST GUARD	Am kopf! *(both burst out laughing)*
2ND GUARD	Ah, Wolf!
1ST GUARD	Ah, Kurt! *(both exiting)*
NARRATOR	Inside the munitions plant, the daring trio, Johnny Canuck, Ruth Barton, and Derek Bras d'Or face an awesome task.

The trio lift up the book flat and turn it around. On the inside of the flat are painted pipes and explosives.

RUTH	This isn't going to be easy. A single hitch and we'll be blown up along with the plant.
JOHNNY	Well, at least we'd be setting Hitler's war effort back a few months. It's worth the risk, but maybe you should leave, Ruth.
RUTH	Don't make me mad, Johnny Canuck. I'm just as capable of handling dangerous situations as you. Besides, how much do you guys know about explosive chemicals? I wasn't sent over here for my good looks, you know.
JOHNNY	Well, me neither.
DEREK	Ruth ne partez pas!

RUTH   Thank you, Derek.

                        RUTH kisses him, making JOHNNY
                        jealous. There is the noise of banging
                        pipes.

RUTH   Listen, the plant is starting a new shift. We must
                        work carefully.

NARRATOR   The daring Canucks are in the final stage of their
                        attempt to blow up the German Munitions plant.
                        As Ruth Barton mixes the explosives, Johnny
                        drills a hole in the metal containers. Above,
                        Derek Bras d'Or, the golden-armed Canadian,
                        keeps watch for Nazi guards.

                        DEREK was looking away, but snaps
                        to attention with the NARRATOR's
                        comment.

RUTH   Okay, Johnny, this will act as our timing device.
                        How long will it take us to clear the plant?

JOHNNY   I'd say three minutes if no one stops us.

RUTH   Okay, let's allow four. Out the front, let's go.

                        They turn the flat back the way it was
                        before.

JOHNNY   Just in time, Ruth. Those horrible Huns are after
                        us now!

RUTH   This way.

                        They quickly run. They are confronted
                        by a spotlight with a swastika sign.
                        They run back.

RUTH   Duck!

                        The light passes over them, and they
                        take a few steps more.

RUTH	Duck! *(as it passes again)* Oh, here it comes again. Johnny, can you get it?
JOHNNY	*(as RUTH gives him a gun from her purse)* Gee, I don't know. It's a tough shot.

> JOHNNY *scores. A technician does a death scream as the light goes out.*

RUTH	Good work!
JOHNNY	That should give us enough cover. Now, let's run across the field.
RUTH	*(as they run)* Wait! Johnny. Stop. The sign.
JOHNNY	What does it say?
RUTH	Derek, stop! Mines. Johnny, this is a mine field! We can't go this way.
JOHNNY	What are we going to do? We can't go through here. We can't go back because the plant will blow up any minute.

> *Suddenly the lights come up.*

DEREK	Bosch! Bosch!

> GUARDS *come from behind the plant and aim their guns at our heroes.*

GUARD	Look, gentlemen of der Turd Reich. Ve haf captured Johnny Canuck and all his friends. Der Fuhrer vill revard us all. Dey are all sitting ducks, nein? Ve vill haf ourselfes some target practice.
RUTH	Oh, Johnny, what can we do?
GUARD	Ready!
DEREK	Maudit Bosch!

JOHNNY   Ruth, I'm afraid this is the end, and I just want to say before I die...

GUARD   Aim!

RUTH   Wait, what time is it?

> *There is a small explosion inside the plant.*

GUARD   Himmel! Vot in der name of Gott iss das?

RUTH   Duck, quick!

> *Then there is a big explosion. The GUARDS fly in the air, knocking down the munitions plant flat. Two "BOOM" signs appear.*

DEREK   *(jumping up and down)* Nyaa, Nyaa, Bosch. Nyaa, Nyaa, Bosch.

JOHNNY   Just in the nick of time. Great engineering, Ruth. Let's go home.

> *The "Hurray" lights come on.*

RUTH   Great Canadian teamwork if I have to say so myself. Hurray for the Canucks! Okay, let's get out of here before the city recovers from shock.

> *They all bump into each other.*

JOHNNY   No, this way!

RUTH   Right. *(running off)*

***

Sc. x. -- REACTION ABROAD

> *A radio microphone with a British emblem is brought out.*

NARRATOR   While Johnny Canuck and the Canadian Supersquad continue to tear at the underbelly of Hitler's Germany, many other European countries crumble under the deadly onslaught of the Axis powers.

> *BRIAN is sitting in a trench listening to a small radio. Enter CHURCHILL, with bowler hat, cigar, and bathrobe.*

CHURCHILL   *(after coughing and clearing his throat)* This is now Britain's darkest hour. Enemy planes continue to strafe our beaches and terrorize the British people. However, we will not give in. Though we have lost our positions in France and Holland and Belgium and Norway and Finland and Luxembourg; though ten million men have been sacrificed and all of our finest ships have been lost to enemy fire; though our allies have given in to the enemy, and though we have no ammunition or supplies to save them; though this is Britain's darkest hour, soon it will become Britain's finest hour. *(off in his own world and visibly salivating)* In history, men will say that I said that though this was our darkest hour, it was also our finest hour. It will be said that I said I offer you nothing but blood, sweat, toil and tears; tears, toil, sweat and blood; and I hope that blood, sweat, toil and tears, will lift us from our present gloom.

> *An English GENTLEMAN enters. He uses his handkerchief to wipe CHURCHILL's mouth.*

GENTLEMAN   Excuse me, Winston, but I have just been
            informed that Johnny Canuck has destroyed the
            Berlin Munitions Factory and that the German
            supply lines are in disarray.

CHURCHILL   Indeed? This is the first good news I have
            received in months.

BOTH   *(showing victory sign)* Hurrah for Johnny
            Canuck!

            BRIAN *turns radio off.*

        ***

Sc. xi. -- DOMESTIC TRAGEDY

        *The setting is the German suburban
            kitchen of* FRAULEIN FANNY VON
            SCHMIDT. *The background shows
            cracks in the plaster but the atmosphere
            is cheery.*

NARRATOR   The story thus far. As Adolf Hitler orders a
            desperate search for Johnny Canuck, the Canadian
            Squad are seeking a place of refuge. Resistance
            member Ricky von Schwinden has brought the
            Canucks to Fraulein Fanny von Schmidt in her
            house in the suburbs of Berlin.

        RICKY *brings* JOHNNY *and* DEREK
            to the house. DEREK *enters first.*

FANNY   Oooooh! my hero! My hero, Johnny Canuck.

        RUTH *runs up and gives* DEREK *a big
            hug which he enjoys.*

RUTH   Oh, you are so big and strong and wonderful.

JOHNNY   Er, excuse me, Fraulein von Schmidt...

FANNY   Please, call me Fanny.

RICKY   This is Johnny Canuck, and this is his friend,
               Derek Bras d'Or. Both great Canadian legends.

FANNY   You? Johnny Canuck? But you're so skinny!

JOHNNY   Gee.

DEREK   I am not zo skinny, Fraulein Fanny. And neider
               are you. *(giggling and slapping her bottom)*

FANNY   Oh you wicked Canadian, you! *(laughing)*

JOHNNY   Say, when did you learn to speak English,
               Derek?

DEREK   Ruth teach me.

JOHNNY   Shucks! I didn't know that.

FANNY   You brave Canadians are all welcome. I am
               sorry, Johnny Canuck, for teasing you. You
               must all sit down, now, and have some milk and
               apfel strudel.

RICKY   Ich muss gehen, Fraulein.

FANNY   You must not go, Ricky.

RICKY   I must go to headquarters and get Ruth.

JOHNNY   Ruth? Maybe I should go too.

RICKY   No, Johnny. It will be safer if I go alone.
               Wiedersehen.

FANNY   Wiedersehen.

DEREK   Bye-bye.

FANNY   Well, what a wonderful day! I have two brave
               Canucks and fresh apfel strudel!

> *Everyone laughs, then freezes with the music.*

NARRATOR As Ricky von Schwinden steps outside, however, an evil glow creeps across his face.

RICKY These Canucks won't be leaving there for a while. I'm fed up with this war. I'm going to help Hitler end it once and for all. If I lead the Gestapo to this house, 10,000 Marks are mine. Good-night, Johnny Canuck, you fool. *(exiting)*

> JOHNNY, DEREK *and* FANNY *break their freeze and continue their laugh.*

DEREK Apple strudel, apple strudel, yum, yum, yum. *(lifting* FANNY *up)*

FANNY Hey, put me down, Golden Arms. *(bringing out the apple strudel)* Now, Johnny, you sit down there. This chair is for you Derek Golden Arms. Alas, there is no chair for me so I might just have to sit on your lap, if you don't mind.

DEREK Comme vous voulez, ma petite fleur!

> JOHNNY *is embarrassed and gets up.*

JOHNNY This sure is a great place you've got here, Fanny. I hope that someday when the war is over, I'll have a nice place like this.

FANNY Maybe you can build one for your girl, Ruth.

JOHNNY Aw, shucks.

DEREK Apple strudel! *(running to* FANNY *and pulling her back onto his lap)*

FANNY Let me go, Golden Arms. Eat your strudel. Yes, I like this little place. Germany would be such a good country if only we could get rid of the Nazis.

There is a knock on the door.

FANNY   Who can that be? Quick, hide in the basement.

FANNY opens the trap door.

RICKY   Fanny! It's me, Ricky.

FANNY   Oh, it's only Ricky. We needn't worry.

FANNY opens the door and RICKY barges in with CORPORAL VON SCHWARZ. Both are armed.

RICKY   There they are, Corporal von Schwarz. The Canucks are all yours.

SCHWARZ   Stay where you are, Canuck. I have you covered.

JOHNNY   Ricky, you traitorous fiend!

FANNY   How could you betray the Resistance, you insect!

RICKY   *(pushing her away)* Don't waste your breath on insults. I hate myself too, so why bother. Besides, I already heard enough insults from Ruth.

JOHNNY   Ruth!

RICKY   I'll get my money in the morning, Schwarz. The Canucks are all yours. *(exiting)*

SCHWARZ   Danke, Ricky. Yes, Ruth Barton is also our prisoner. Now we have captured all the Canucks. *(menacing FANNY)* But you, traitor to der Turd Reich. You dare to harbour dese enemies of der Fatterland. You vill meet der same fate as your cousin, Otto, der miserable dog ve killed in a previous episode. *(pointing his gun)*

DEREK   Maudit Bosch!

> DEREK *attacks* SCHWARZ *who fires a heavy volley of machine gun fire.* DEREK *is hit and stunned.* FANNY *screams.* JOHNNY *attacks* SCHWARZ *and grapples the gun from his hands. A blow with rifle butt sends* SCHWARZ *sprawling.*

JOHNNY   This should end your career, you lowdown snake. *(firing into* SCHWARZ, *who screams and dies)*

FANNY   *(near* DEREK, *who has fallen)* Johnny, come quick. Derek is very sick.

JOHNNY   Derek, my old friend. How are you?

DEREK   J'ai mal, mon ami.

JOHNNY   You'll pull through, a tough Canadian woodsman like you. We'll get a doctor.

DEREK   Pas de docteur, Johnny. Ou est ma petite fleur?

FANNY   I'm here, mein liebchen.

DEREK   Tu es tres belle, petite fleur. I no look so good, no?

FANNY   No, my Golden Arms. You look so funny before, now you look sad. *(crying)*

DEREK   Ne pleures pas, petite fleur. Je suis content. I die for you, non? Johnny, tuez tous les Bosch. *(tickling* FANNY's *chin)* Moi, Golden Arms! *(laughing)* Maudit Bosch!

> DEREK *dies.* FANNY *cannot speak. She buries her head on* DEREK's *shoulder.*

JOHNNY   A brave sacrifice, Derek. Like so many of those
                brave Canadian soldiers. I'll find you, Ruth. Well
                get you yet, Adolf! The Canucks are not finished
                yet!!

                        *Grand music as the lights fade and the
                        curtain closes.*

NARRATOR   We'll take a short break now, but be sure to
                return to our next adventure when Johnny
                Canuck meets Adolf Hitler face to face!

                        ***

ACT TWO

Sc. xii. --- THE ARRIVAL OF MAJOR DOMO

                        *The scene is an underground hideout,
                        but can be played easily in front of the
                        curtain.*

NARRATOR   We return you to the adventures of Johnny
                Canuck and the Canadian Supersquad. The story
                thus far: A treacherous betrayal in the resistance
                movement has lead to the capture of the lovely
                Ruth Barton and the death of the heroic Derek
                Bras d'Or. Johnny awaits the arrival of Major
                Domo, an unusual new superhero.

                        MAJOR DOMO *makes his entrance. He
                        has an old-fashioned European jacket on.
                        His sleeves are buttoned up so that it is
                        obvious that he has no arms.* JOHNNY
                        *is about to shake his hand, when he
                        stops.*

DOMO   You noticed. Yes, I lost my arms in the Great
                War fighting the Bosch then. And I have been
                fighting a war against Fascism ever since and
                will continue until all men have an equal share of
                the world's resources.

JOHNNY

Gee, I appreciate your courage, Major Domo, but this is a desperate situation. We need a man with arms of steel to tear down the Nazi fortresses and rescue Ruth Barton.

DOMO

No offense, Johnny Canuck, but what you need is a man of imagination, a man with a giant brain. That man is me. I know Berlin like the back of my hand -- no jokes, please -- and I will design a plan that will get your Ruth. Now be quiet while I think of a plan. *(banging his head against the wall with a great thrust three times)*

JOHNNY

I hope Dixon knows what he's doing.

DOMO

I've got it! We must get you inside Hitler's Chancellory.

JOHNNY

But how?

DOMO

Silence! I'm thinking. *(banging his head three more times)* I have it! I will show you how to get a uniform and then draw you a map of the Chancellory. I would do it myself, but I am a little difficult to disguise. But first, you must become a Nazi.

JOHNNY

What? Me, a Nazi? Never!

DOMO

It's only a disguise, Johnny Canuck. Now, I will be the German sentry. You walk up to me, salute and I will ask you for your papers.

JOHNNY

Okay, sounds easy.

> JOHNNY *does a stiff walk towards* DOMO.

DOMO

Papers, please.

JOHNNY

Oh, sure, here they are.

DOMO   No, no! There are only two things to remember
                about being a German. Walk like a machine and
                bark like a dog. I will show you.

                        They trade places, and DOMO *does a*
                        very rigid walking goosestep. He thrusts
                        his shoulder stump forward.

DOMO   Sieg heil!

JOHNNY   Papers.

DOMO   Papers? You miserable dog! You dare to ask an
                officer of the Third Reich for papers! You cur!
                You miserable schwein! *(stepping past the guard)*
                You see?

JOHNNY   Got it! *(to himself)* Walk like a machine, bark
                like a dog. *(marching up)* Sieg heil!

DOMO   Your papers please.

JOHNNY   Who are you asking for papers, you miserable
                dog --

DOMO   *(jumping up)* Who are you calling a dog, you
                dog?

                        DOMO *and* JOHNNY *both start barking*
                        at each other furiously, reaching a
                        crescendo..

DOMO   Good! *(as* JOHNNY *stops)* But your accent is
                terrible. Come, we work on it. Now march some
                more.

                        They go off, marching and barking
                        together.

                            ***

Sc. xiii. -- INSIDE HITLER'S CHANCELLORY THE TABLES TURN

NARRATOR Having broken the back of the German Resistance Movement, Adolf Hitler rests comfortably in his heavily guarded office, confident that victory is close at hand.

> HITLER *reads a Superman comic book. There is a knock on the door.*

HITLER Password.

GOEBBELS I forget, mein Fuhrer.

HITLER Come in, Gobbles.

> GOEBBELS *enters with* RUTH, *trips on the way in.*

GOEBBELS I fell over, mein Fuhrer. Gut morgen mein Fuhrer, you are going to be very proud of me this morning, mein Fuhrer. I haf here Ruth Barton, one of der silly leaders of der silly underground. Now dat ve haf her, ve vill be able to lay a very nice trap for dat scoundrel John Canuck.

HITLER How many times must I inform you, Josef, do not mention dat name when I am reading my comics. You know what to do. Get all de information from her by any means you deem just.

GOEBBELS You mean I should turn her over to Black Hans?

BOTH Heh, heh, heh.

RUTH Adolf, you silly ass!

GOEBBELS *(aside)* Vot nerve, vot pluck! How often haf I vished to say just that myself.

RUTH
(driving HITLER *on top of his desk)* You are fools to think you can destroy the Resistance Movement. After my demise, Johnny will rally thousands of volunteers to avenge my death. So, beware, Adolf baby, you are no match for Johnny Canuck.

HITLER
Gobbles, Gobbles, save me from dis insane voman. Shoot her, Josef, shoot her, I beg you.

GOEBBELS
But, mein Fuhrer, you said to get information from her.

HITLER
Nein, nein, shoot her, shoot her.

GOEBBELS
Couldn't ve just turn her over to Black Hans, heh, heh, heh?

HITLER
Nein, shoot her right now!!

GOEBBEIS
Yes, mein Fuhrer *(he can't find his gun)* Could I borrow one of yours? So! Goot-bye, Ruth Barton and join der fate of all der other silly Canucks.

RUTH
Long live democracy! Death to all Fascists.

Knock on the door.

GOEBBELS
There's someone at der door, mein Fur.

HITLER
Password.

JOHNNY
What shall I say? *(peeking through the props curtain at the audience)*

GOEBBELS
What did he say?

HITLER
Password!

JOHNNY
I forget, mein Fuhrer.

GOEBBELS
Ah, it's only me, mein Fuhrer.

> GOEBBELS *lets* JOHNNY
> *in, goosestepping.*

JOHNNY   Baron von Richter at your service, mein Fur.

HITLER   Vot is your news? Have you got dat scoundrel Canuck?

JOHNNY   Alas, mein Fur. Johnny Canuck has escaped and is apparently on his way here to rescue Ruth Barton.

HITLER   Oooooh! Oooooh! Gobbles, shoot dis girl immediately.

JOHNNY   Aaahh. *(pushing* GOEBBELS *aside)* This must be the lovely Ruth Barton. If you will permit ein suggestion, mein Fur, it is rumoured that Johnny Canuck is in love with this girl and as long as she is alive she is the perfect bait to lure Johnny Canuck into a trap once and for all.

RUTH   No, kill me. I will not be a part of a plan to kill Johnny.

JOHNNY   Mein Fur, I think maybe she is in love with dat Canuck herself. It is rumoured Canuck will penetrate the Chancellory by the back gate. Perhaps the guard should be warned?

GOEBBELS   *(to* HITLER*)* Don't you think the guard should be warned?

HITLER   Don't you think you'd better go and warn?

GOEBBELS   Mein Fuhrer, I'm going to warn the guards. *(tripping)* I'm always falling...*(exiting)*

HITLER   Oooohh. I vish I had dat Canuck right here in dis office, I vould, I vould, I vould.

> JOHNNY *is whispering something into* RUTH's *ear, she then recognizes him.*

RUTH	It's Johnny!
HITLER	Vait, vait a minute, you don't valk like a Cherman.

JOHNNY takes off his hat.

HITLER	You valk more like Johnny Canuck!!
JOHNNY	That's right, Adolf old chap. I've been waiting for this moment for a long time.
RUTH	Oh Johnny, thank goodness you're here.
JOHNNY	I hope you didn't doubt me, Ruth.
HITLER	Vat are you going to do? Please, Johnny, be a good boy, don't hurt me. I never really meant any harm.
JOHNNY	You wouldn't think this worm commanded a giant army now, would you, Ruth?
HITLER	Everybody has their bad days. *(as RUTH laughs)* It's not enough you break in here and destroy my war machine, but if you make fun of me, I vill haf to do something desperate.

HITLER lunges for a gun. JOHNNY grabs him, but the gun goes off. JOHNNY pins HITLER's sleeve to the desk with a knife.

RUTH	Good work, Johnny.
JOHNNY	Another move like that, Adolf, and it will be your last.

JOHNNY and RUTH hide behind the door, as GOEBBELS comes rushing in, gun pointed.

GOEBBELS	Ahh! Mein Fuhrer, vot is der matter?

HITLER	How dare you enter mit out giffing der password!
GOEBBELS	I forgot, mein Fuhrer. I mean, I thought that maybe you had shot yourself.
HITLER	Me, shot myself. Idiot, ven I shot myself, you vill be der first to know. You fool, ve haf a guest!
GOEBBELS	Ja? Oh, dat's nice. Who iss?
JOHNNY	*(pointing a gun in his back)* Johnny Canuck, Gobble-gook.
GOEBBELS	Johnny Canuck! Johnny Canuck! Da really Johnny Canuck? Oh, mein Herr Canuck, vill you autograph dis comic book for me? Just write, to dear Gobbles, mit --
HITLER	NOT NOW, IDIOT! *(on the phone)* Send in der guard!
JOHNNY	Oh, a trick, eh?
	JOHNNY *K.O.'s* GOEBBELS *who goes flying across the stage. A big* GUARD *comes in. He and* JOHNNY *face off but the* GUARD *is so stupid he practically flops on to the floor by himself. As he and* JOHNNY *wrestle,* HITLER *tiptoes away.*
HITLER	Goot-bye.
RUTH	*(grabbing him by the hair)* Oh no you don't, Adolf.
	RUTH *uses him like a punching bag and* HITLER *collapses.* JOHNNY *is still struggling with the* GUARD *who keeps making gurgling noises.*

JOHNNY   Boy, you sure are tough for a German. *(using a gun to knock him out)* Okay, who's next?

                              GOEBBELS *rushes in to* JOHNNY *on his knees.*

GOEBBELS   Oh no, Mister Canuck, please don't hurt me.

                              JOHNNY's *gun is accidentally knocked towards* HITLER, *who snatches it.*

HITLER   Aha!

GOEBBELS   *(getting up and grabbing another gun)* Aha! *(standing in front of* HITLER's *gun and then kicked aside)*

HITLER   Don't moof, Canuck. Vun more step and I vill fire. Now, Canuck, to end your worthless life once and for all!

NARRATOR   Will the treacherous fiend, Adolf Hitler, kill our hero, Johnny Canuck? Watch!

GUARD   *(waking up)* Ach! Mein head.

                              GUARD *looks around, gets the picture, then bursts out laughing.* ADOLF *and* GOEBBELS *look at each other and laugh with him. Then* ADOLF *quickly shoots the* GUARD *who stops laughing and dies immediately.*

HITLER   Idiot! So der Fuhrer triumphs over der Canucks once more! *(pointing gun)* No, wait. You haf insulted der Fuhrer of der Turd Reich. Death is not enough punishment!

GOEBBELS   Maybe we could turn dem over to Black Hans.

BOTH   Heh, heh, heh!

HITLER   Yes, Black Hans. A Cherman specialty. Der
                Canucks vill die a cruel death in der public square
                at der hands of Black Hans!

JOHNNY
& RUTH   Oh, no!

HITLER &
GOEBBELS   Oh, yes!

***

Sc. xiv. -- THE ARMS OF MAJOR DOMO

                *The underground hideout; this too, can
                be played in front of the curtain.*

NARRATOR   Back at the Canadian hideout, Major Domo, the
                arm-less hero, hears the news of Canuck's capture
                on the radio.

DOMO   *(looking up with alarm)* Et tu, Canuck? Another
                Nazi victim? I have failed. My plan has failed! 0
                miserable, woeful, blasted day, that I should see
                the Canucks in such disarray! Ooooohhh!
                (banging his head on the wall three times) They
                will laugh at me and tell me I have failed. Me,
                Major Domo, the greatest Nazi repellent the
                world has ever known. Oh why did I have to lose
                my arms? *(with classic style)* That fateful day on
                Vimy Ridge, when all the shutters of the world
                closed in on me. I was the first to climb the hill;
                I planted the flag for the glory of Canada, and
                then, the terrible blast that severed my limbs
                from my body and left me but a shadow of my
                former self. O, must I remember!? *(banging his
                head three times on the floor)* If only I had arms!
                I would rescue you Johnny Canuck, and you too
                Ruth Barton. My nose for a pair of arms! My
                liver for a pair of arms! My -- *(looking down)* --
                legs for a pair of arms. Oh blast! blast! blast!

                Soft music and a knock on the door.

DOMO	*(suspicious)* Ja?
MARIO	*(voice offstage)* Signor Domo?
DOMO	Ja?
MARIO	Signor Dominique Domino Domo?
DOMO	Who wants to know?
MARIO	*(with a funny mustache, bright Mafiosi clothes, waddles in briskly, carrying a box with a ribbon)* My name is Mario, and I have brought you a present from a mutual friend, Professor Gassi.
DOMO	Gassi? I thought he was killed by the Italian Fascists.
MARIO	Oh no, fortunato, he escaped and carries on the resistance work against the evils of the Benito Mussolini Axis. Please, open your gift.
DOMO	What is it?
MARIO	Open it. Oh, excuse me, I will help.
DOMO	Domo does not need help. *(undoing the string with his teeth)*
MARIO	There! What do you think of that?
DOMO	I...I...I don't understand.
MARIO	*(with musical accompaniment, pulling out two colourful arms)* You like?
DOMO	Is this some kind of joke?
MARIO	No, no. Special for you. Work like new. Very strong. Guaranteed. Please you try them on.
DOMO	No! Domo does not need arms.

MARIO   I no doubt it. But with these arms, you will carry Johnny Canuck out of the hands of the Nazis.

DOMO   Canuck? Okay, I will try them on. But I don't promise.

MARIO   Here you are, one arm, and now another arm, and here, no jacket, this will make you feel less self-conscious. *(putting a cape over* DOMO*)* Covers up the joints. Oh! Signor Domo, you look so handsome. *(to audience)* Don't he look handsome? *(to* DOMO*)* You know, I have a very pretty sister in Italy who is not yet married...

DOMO   I can't move them. What's wrong?

MARIO   O qual stupido, I forget to activate them. Uno momento. *(taking one hand and whispering into the fingers, "Uno, Due, Tre"; with the effect of blowing into a microphone)*

DOMO   Are you talking to my fingers?

MARIO   Ho, ho, how amusing. No, I was only counting them. All five fingers there, now, ready to activate. *(blowing again into fingers)* Activate now!

> MARIO *kicks* DOMO's *posterior. There is weird music and the arms start to move.*

DOMO   They move! They work! They are working! I have arms. Domo has arms.

MARIO   Si! Incredible, no?

DOMO   *(marching proudly)* Let me shake your hand, Signor Mario.

MARIO   *(stepping aside)* I am honoured, Signor, but I must go now.

DOMO   My hand isn't good enough for you?

MARIO   No, itsa not that...

DOMO   Please, your hand! *(grabbing* MARIO's *hand and squeezing very hard)*

MARIO   No, no. Signor Domo, please, it is too tight!

DOMO   Thank you, Signor Mario. *(opening his arms wide)*

MARIO   Nooooo! (as DOMO *squeezing him)* No! *(choking)*

DOMO   And now, you must excuse me. I have important things to do. *(in a superhero pose)* Look out, you sauerkrauts! Domo has arms! *(dashing off)*

MARIO   *(slowly crawling to the wall and taking out a walkie talkie)* Allo, Roma! Uno due tre. Allo Roma. Allo, Mussolini, Ahh, Benito! Allo, Mio Duce. Domo is programmed to kidnap Canuck, si, the plan, she worked, except for one minor detail...*(choking and dying)*

                              ***

Sc. xv. -- CANADIAN BLOOD ON THE NAZI GUILLOTINE

NARRATOR   On a grim day in history, Adolf Hitler gleefully awaits the public execution of Johnny Canuck and Ruth Barton. A barbarous death has been planned by Hitler's pride and joy, Black Hans.

                The curtain opens to reveal a guillotine and BLACK HANS, *dressed in a mail shirt and a black hood. The crowd is cheering his arrival.*

BLACK HANS   Today, man, you gonna see dese Canucks heads roll.

>JOHNNY *and* RUTH *are pushed on stage.* RUTH *has a new elegant outfit on.*

RUTH　　　　Oh look, Johnny. It's a guillotine.

JOHNNY　　　It's too gruesome for words, Ruth. If only there was some way to get you away from these barbarians.

RUTH　　　　No, Johnny, if you're going to die, then I want to die with you.

JOHNNY　　　Ruth!

RUTH　　　　Johnny!

JOHNNY　　　Ruth!

RUTH　　　　Johnny!

BLACK HANS　All right, I want you cats to look this way. I want you Canucks to see what I'm gonna do to you. Now you feel this blade *(pulling* JOHNNY'*s arm to the blade)* You feel it! Sharp, eh? Sharp enough to slice a tomato in two, eh? And you see this, this is where you lie down, now you watch while I demonstrate for you. *(down on the guillotine)* See, now this is where your head goes, facing up, German style. *(getting up)* And when I pull this string, it chop your head off. You listen to the sound of the blade coming down. *(dropping the blade)* You like dat? *(laughing)* And now, I suppose you're curious about where your head go to? *(opening up the trap door and pointing to a red bucket)* You like dat?

JOHNNY　　　You black fiend! Why can't you just shoot us and let us die a soldier's death?

>*Enter* HITLER *and* GOEBBELS.

HITLER	Because dat vould be too easy, Johnny Canuck. You haf caused der Turd Reich a great deal of distress, but now you are an example to der vorld of der German triumph of vill over mere Canadian courage.
JOHNNY	Don't worry, Ruth, history will be on our side.
BLACK HANS	Can I start now, mein Fuhrer?
HITLER	Yes, Black Hans. Begin der chopping down of two more Canadian legends. Goot-bye forever, Johnny Canuck and Ruth Barton.
GOEBBELS	This way, mein Fuhrer. I haf reserved two seats for us in der balcony.

HITLER *and* GOEBBELS *exit.*

JOHNNY	Oh, Ruth, this looks like the end, and I just want to say before I die, that I, that I, well, I love you, Ruth.
RUTH	*(very loudly over the music)* And I love you too, Johnny. Oh, if only there was something we could do.
BLACK HANS	Okay, which one of you is going first?
JOHNNY	I'll go first.
RUTH	Oh, Johnny, please let me. I couldn't bear to look.
JOHNNY	Very well, Ruth, if that is your last wish.

RUTH *puts her purse on the side of the guillotine, then lies down.*

BLACK HANS	That's right, she was a good girl, she was watching...
RUTH	Good-bye, Johnny. Good-bye, Canada.

Drum roll.

BLACK HANS   Look at me, Mister Canuck, you look this way! Are you ready, mein Fuhrer?

GOEBBELS   *(offstage)* Der Fuhrer is ready.

Drum roll intensifies.

BLACK HANS   Ein. Zwei. I said look this way, Mister Canuck!

JOHNNY   Good-bye, Ruth.

BLACK HANS   Drei.

HANS *drops the blade, but suddenly* MAJOR DOMO *leaps up from the trap door and stops the blade a few inches away from* RUTH's *neck.*

JOHNNY   Domo!

DOMO   Look out, you Nazis! Domo has arms!

BLACK HANS   Hey, man, what do you think

Cymbals sound as DOMO *punches* HANS.

JOHNNY   *(rushing forward)* I must do something. *(straining at his ropes and pulling them apart)* Ah, they'd better start making stronger rope if they want to hold Canadians captive! *(as he unties* RUTH*)* Okay, Ruth, let's get out of here.

RUTH   Wait, my purse.

RUTH *and* JOHNNY *exit.*

DOMO   *(as he backs* HANS *towards the guillotine, punching him all the way with cymbal sounds)* Domo has arms! Domo has arms! Domo has arms!

BLACK HANS   *(on the guillotine)* No, no, please Domo.!

> *HANS's head is pushed under the blade.*
> *As the blade drops, the actor lets his*
> *black hood fall into the red bucket.*

DOMO   Hurray for Major Domo! *(running off)*

> *RUTH and JOHNNY re-enter, with*
> *pistols.*

JOHNNY   We're surrounded by thousands of Nazis. How
will we ever get out of here?

> *There is a bugle sound, and DIXON*
> *rides on to the stage on a two-*
> *dimensional horse, complete with a*
> *Canadian flag on its rear.*

JOHNNY   Ruth! Look!

DIXON   What's all this noise? By tar, it's Johnny and
Ruth. I'll fire into the crowd and disperse those
Nazis. *(as JOHNNY and RUTH join in the fire)*
Climb aboard.

> *They all mount the horse.*

DOMO   *(re-emerging)* This way, I've found a secret exit.

> *Suddenly DIXON is hit and the*
> *shooting stops.*

RUTH   Dixon!

DIXON   It's okay. It's only a shoulder wound. *(as they
move off and continue the fire)*

ALL   Hurray for the Canucks!

> *The lights are flashing and the music is*
> *triumphant.*

Sc. xvi. -- TREACHERY WITHIN THE RANKS

NARRATOR   The story thus far. Dixon and Domo, the latter
now wielding --

> *The curtains open and we see the set
> change still in progress. The actors are
> caught. There is a moment, then the
> curtains close. To cover the pause, the
> NARRATOR sings "Lady of Spain".
> The curtains open. They are still not
> ready. Curtains close and the
> NARRATOR sings another verse. The
> curtains open once more and everyone is
> in a lovely freeze pose.*

NARRATOR   Thank you. The story thus far. Dixon and Domo,
the latter now wielding a pair of mysterious
arms, have rescued Johnny and Ruth from the
guillotine. In the battle, however, Dixon has
been wounded. He now rests comfortably in the
underground headquarters, nursed by Ruth Barton.

> *DOMO is doing a tango.*

RUTH   Please, Domo, we must let Corporal Dixon rest
in peace.

DOMO   It's just a shoulder wound. I want to dance to
celebrate. *(dancing a wild tango)*

JOHNNY   I think you should stop dancing and behave like a
Canadian, Domo.

DOMO   Hey, don't boss me around, Canuck. I've got
arms now and I want to dance. *(dancing more)*

RUTH   Oh, come on, Major Domo.

DIXON   That's enough. Everyone be quiet.

DOMO   Listen, Corporal --

DIXON
I said be quiet, Major Domo. We all appreciate your heroism today, but you are all on a special assignment and must behave with Canadian modesty. *(coughing profusely)*

RUTH
Are you okay, Dixon?

DIXON
One good night's sleep under the stars and I should be my old self again. Your work in Germany has gone well and everyday we come closer to scoring the defeat of Fascism in Europe.

RUTH *and* JOHNNY *applaud. So does* DOMO.

JOHNNY
However -- *(applause stops)* a major new threat has arisen which it seems only the Canadians can conquer.

JOHNNY
What is it, Dixon, we can do it.

RUTH
Yes, we're ready for more.

DIXON
I'm afraid it's the lowdown Japanese who now control the South Pacific and are threatening our friends, the Chinese. We must destroy the Nips once and for all. Think you can handle it, Johnny?

JOHNNY
(curling his lip) Sure.

DIXON
Ruth, you must help our Commie friends lift the siege of Stalingrad, got it?

RUTH
You bet.

DIXON
Major Domo, you will maintain the underground momentum in Germany until we reunite. Any questions?

RUTH
Oh, Johnny, this means we must separate.

JOHNNY Yes, Ruth, but when the war is over, perhaps, perhaps we need never separate again.

DOMO Your plan, Corporal Dixon, I don't like it.

DIXON *(with a patronizing laugh)* My plan is not a proposal, Major; it is a direct order from Mackenzie King himself.

DOMO I think we should go to Italy and --

DIXON Domo, these orders are final. Ruth, will you make us some tea?

DOMO Allow me, Ruth, it will be good exercise for my arms. *(exiting)*

RUTH What's making Domo so irritable today?

JOHNNY He sure is strange.

DIXON Well, he's a cripple, Ruth...

DOMO *(entering with two-dimensional cups)* Cocoa, everyone! Pretty quick with my new arms, eh?

ALL Gee, thanks, Domo.

DOMO Drink up. I will be insulted if you don't drink. After all, it's the first cocoa I've ever made since the last war.

DIXON *(finishing it)* And good cocoa it is too, Domo.

JOHNNY Well, Domo, do you think you can manage the Underground without us?

DOMO Of course. I can handle anything. But I don't like it. We shouldn't separate --

DIXON We haven't time to argue. All missions must be successful or -- *(staggering)* I feel dizzy, something's wrong.

DOMO	Drink your cocoa. It will make you better. Ruth, you haven't been drinking.
JOHNNY	I'm feeling dizzy myself.
RUTH	Maybe we should all just go to bed. *(rising and dropping cup)*
DOMO	Ruth, you stupid girl! How dare you spill the cocoa. That was my cocoa. I'll fix you. You spilled it on purpose. *(throwing a chair aside)*
RUTH	Domo! Stop him Johnny.
JOHNNY	Domo, stop it.

> JOHNNY *rushes forward, but* DOMO *knocks him aside.*

JOHNNY	I can't see straight.
RUTH	It's the cocoa. There's something wrong with the cocoa. Domo, please stop.
DOMO	I'll fix you all. No one can stop me. I am the leader here. I am the only true superman. All who oppose me will die. Ruth will die first.

> DOMO *advances on* RUTH *who runs to* DIXON *and takes his gun and shoots at* DOMO*'s arms.*

DOMO	My arms. She wants to destroy my arms. No! I need my arms. *(going on a rampage, lifting the table high above his head)*
RUTH	Johnny, Dixon, wake up, it's Domo's arms. There must be something wrong with his arms. Quick!

> DIXON *and* JOHNNY *struggle to revive themselves.*

DOMO	I am invincible. I am invincible!
JOHNNY	Grab his arms. Grab his arms!

> Johnny *grabs one arm,* DIXON *and* RUTH *the other. They pull.*

DOMO   No! Nnnoooo! My arms. What are you doing? NOOO! NOOO! NOOOOO! PLEASE, DOOOON'T!

> *There is a flash as the arms are pulled out of* DOMO's *sockets.* DOMO *becomes as gentle as a pussycat.*

DOMO   *(after a pause)* Where am I?

JOHNNY   Look, there's a transmitter in the socket. Domo, I think you were tricked. I'm -- I'm -- what's happening?

> DIXON *and* JOHNNY *collapse on the floor.*

DOMO   Poison! I've poisoned them! Quick, Ruth, get the antidote.

> RUTH *rushes to the prop closet where someone hands her an antidote.*

RUTH   *(as she rushes to* JOHNNY *and* DIXON *and pours the antidote)* Oh dear, I hope we're not too late.

> *Suspenseful music, then* DIXON *and* JOHNNY *pull themselves up.*

DIXON & JOHNNY   Where am I?

DOMO   Thank goodness! I would never have forgiven myself. What did I do?

JOHNNY   You really didn't do anything, Domo, except
                become an unwilling tool of the Italian Fascists.

DOMO   How stupid I was. Will you forgive me?
                (banging his head on the wall)

RUTH   Poor Major Domo.

DIXON   Dictators certainly know how to turn people into
                machines and monsters. Don't be angry with
                yourself, Major. We've got a lot of noble work
                ahead of us, mopping up the last of the Axis
                menace.

DOMO   You're right. I'll continue the German
                Underground until the Nazis are destroyed. But
                tell me, wasn't it nice, I mean, didn't I look good
                with arms, even if only for a single day?

JOHNNY
RUTH & DIXON Aaaaawww!

> DOMO *smiles sheepishly.*

> ***

Sc. xvii -- COMING HOME

> *The family scene with the radio in front
> of the curtain, on one side of the stage.*

NARRATOR   As the long war finally draws to a close, the
                family anxiously waits for news of loved ones
                overseas.

MOM   This war's supposed to be over, but there are still
                reports of fighting. We haven't heard from Brian
                for so long. Now where can he be?

POP   Well, maybe he was having such a good time, he
                didn't want it to be over.

MOM	Oh you and your comic books.
	There is a knock on the door.
MESSENGER	Overseas Cablegram for Mrs. Russell.
MOM	Overseas cable? What could it be? *(taking the cable and slowly opening it and reading)* "Tell Paw to kill a big rooster. I'm coming home. Love, Brian."
NARRATOR	*(as POP mouths the words in the cable)* Alf Russell just couldn't say a word. He was too pleased to speak and when words choke, well, let 'em choke.
MOM	I think you will agree, dear, that this is one of the happiest days of our lives.
	The curtains part and they exit into the sun. The sun opens up, and they walk right through it. BRIAN enters and rests at the other corner of the stage. He is wearing a dirty army uniform. Enter JOHNNY CANUCK.
JOHNNY	Hi, there, son. Just getting back from the action line, eh?
BRIAN	Yeah, got a cigarette?
JOHNNY	No, sorry, I don't -- What's your name, son?
BRIAN	Brian Russell. *(offers his hand)* Say, you look familiar.
JOHNNY	Yes, a lot of people say that. I've been in a lot of action lines myself these past few years.
BRIAN	Say, maybe I saw you in Dieppe, no? Singapore?
JOHNNY	No, I wasn't with any one of those divisions.

BRIAN	Did you get wounded?
JOHNNY	No, actually, but I sure had some pretty close calls.
BRIAN	Are you sure you weren't crawling in the mud with me in Normandy?
JOHNNY	No, you don't understand. I was on special assignment. You see, *(striking a pose)* I'm Johnny Canuck.
BRIAN	Oh yeah. You're the guy that fought all his battles on the home front. *(exiting abruptly)*
JOHNNY	Now look here...No, I give that kid credit. Those boys fought a great war. Well, think I'll move on. *(moving off)*

CAPTAIN AMERICA *enters with great aplomb and stops him.*

AMERICA	Shazam! Hey, guy, don't cross my path. I'm Captain America.
JOHNNY	Yeah, I can see that. Please to meet you.
AMERICA	I'll bet. Who are you?
JOHNNY	I'm Johnny Canuck.
AMERICA	Yeah? Is that your uniform? *(guffaws of laughter)*
JOHNNY	Well, at least it's Canadian.
AMERICA	Come on, guy, tell me what you did in the War?
JOHNNY	Well, I -- No, it wasn't much. I did my bit, but I'd like to just say it was a great team effort.
AMERICA	*(producing a grand, colourful comic book)* Well, I can tell you what I did in full colour.

AMERICA	*(continued)* It was Captain America that won the war, not the Brits, not the old Allies. We saved their skins in Europe and we wiped the Pacific clean. And we don't mind taking credit for what we done.
JOHNNY	Yeah, well, we'll see you around.
AMERICA	You sure will. Shazam! *(exiting)*
JOHNNY	Well, I guess it's time to get Ruth and plan our trip up north to the woods.

                      Enter DIXON *as if fighting the blizzard.*

JOHNNY	Corporal Dixon!
DIXON	Uh uh, John. *(pointing to his new stripe)* Sergeant, now!
JOHNNY	Sergeant Dixon! Well, congratulations, Sergeant. *(slapping his shoulder)*
DIXON	Ohh! Watch that shoulder, John.
JOHNNY	Sorry, Dixon. Where you off to now?
DIXON	Oh, I'm on a new assignment. Seems that someone's been messing with the Indian moose traps in the Northwest Territories and I've got to find out who and why. In fact, I've got to be off now. So long, Johnny. *(walking off still fighting his blizzard)*
JOHNNY	So long, Sergeant Dixon.

                      DOMO *enters from behind.*

JOHNNY	Major Domo! Are you heading off in a hurry too?

DOMO   Yes, Johnny, I too must run. I am working on a relief ship to save the war victims in Poland. Gotta help get those countries back on their feet. Johnny Canuck, good luck! *(exiting)*

JOHNNY   Good luck to you too, Domo. Keep up that fighting spirit!

         RUTH *enters wearing white blouse and Red Cross cap, and a nice pointed bra.*

JOHNNY   Ruth! You're here.

RUTH   Yes, Johnny, but not for long.

JOHNNY   But Ruth, I thought -- I thought that, with the war being over, I could start building that little house, and that...maybe you'd. Ruth!

RUTH   Yes, Johnny, I know. But I can't. Oh, Johnny, I want that house with the birds and the flowers and the trees...

JOHNNY   Well, I can --

RUTH   But I can't just yet. I have too much important work to do with the Red Cross, helping the suffering and the sick. But when we've finally gotten rid of all the evils of the world and my humanitarian work is finished, then I will want that house, Johnny. Goodbye, Johnny. *(kissing him on the cheek, moving away, waving)* Goodbye. *(then exiting)*

JOHNNY   Well, guess there's just me left. *(taking off his JOHNNY CANUCK sweater)* Think I'll go back to being plain old John Campbell for a while. I'll head up to those great timberlines of Northern Ontario on my own.

         JOHNNY *moves towards the sun.* DEREK's *old lumberjack song is heard in the wings.*

JOHNNY   Ahh, shucks, I'm really going to miss you, Derek.

> JOHNNY *hangs his sweater on the sun, which opens for him, and walks into the horizon. During the next speech, he walks on the spot, but gradually lowering himself until he sinks below the stage forever.*

NARRATOR   Johnny Canuck has not disappeared. You can still find him swinging his axe in Northern Ontario. He is not dead. And if the Fascist Menace ever returns, you can count on Johnny Canuck to save the day. Hurray for Johnny Canuck!

> *Music fit for a great closing.*

> *The End.*

THE KOMAGATA MARU INCIDENT

SHARON POLLOCK

Winner of the Governor General's Award for *Blood Relations* in 1982, Sharon Pollock has written numerous plays for stage, radio and television. She has been Artistic Director at Theatre Calgary and Theatre New Brunswick as well as playwright-in-residence at the National Arts Centre and Alberta Theatre Projects, and also head of the Banff Centre Playwrights Colony for four years. Her other plays include *Doc, Walsh, A Compulsory Option, One Tiger to a Hill, Whiskey Six Cadenza,* and a number of childrens' plays. Sharon Pollock lives in Calgary.

The Komagata Maru Incident was first produced at the Vancouver Playhouse in January, 1976, with the following cast:

T.S	*Allan Stratton*
HOPKINSON	*Richard Fowler*
EVY	*Heather Brechin*
GEORG	*Leroy Schulz*
SOPHIE	*Nicola Cavendish*
WOMAN	*Diana Belshaw*

Directed by Larry Lillo.
Designed by Jack Simon.
Stage Managed by Paul Reynolds.

The Komagat Maru Incident was subsequently produced by Citadel Theatre, Edmonton, in January, 1977, with the following cast:

T.S.	*Ray Hunt*
HOPKINSON	*Michael Ball*
EVY	*Peggy Mahon*
GEORG	*Jean-Pierre Fournier*
SOPHIE	*Angela Gann*
WOMAN	*Patricia Lenyre*

Directed by James DeFelice.
Designed by David Lovett.
Stage Managed by Marion Brant.

PLAYWRIGHT'S INTRODUCTION

The Komagata Maru Incident is a theatrical impression of an historical event seen through the *optique* of the stage and the mind of the playwright. It is not a documentary account, although much of it is documented. To encompass these facts, time and place are often compressed, and certain dramatic licence is employed.

By the early 1900s, the Canadian government believed it had devised an airtight method to virtually exclude immigration from Asia. In 1914, the *Komagata Maru*, a Japanese steamer, entered Vancouver Harbour carrying 376 potential immigrants of East Indian origin. The majority were veterans of the British Army, and all were British subjects. As such, they had right of entry to Canada guaranteed by their membership in the British Empire, but they were forbidden entry by Canadian immigration officials. For the following two months, the Komagata Maru lay at anchor in Burrard Inlet, with those aboard suffering much deprivation, while political, legal, and racial skirmishes ensued. Inspector William Hopkinson of the Department of Immigration was instrumental in negotiations with those aboard and was involved in the formation of a ring of informers within the Sikh community.

The *Komagata Maru* returned to India in the fall of 1914, leaving behind only twenty passengers who could prove former residence in Canada. The repercussions of the government's actions -- the Budge Budge riot, the radicalization of those aboard, the vigilante action against informers, the death of Hopkinson, the execution of Mewa Singh -- were overshadowed by the outbreak of World War One.

As a Canadian, I feel that much of our history has been misrepresented and even hidden from us. Until we recognize our past, we cannot change our future.

Sharon Pollock

THE CHARACTERS

T.S.	The Master of Ceremonies, who plays many roles.
WILLIAM HOPKINSON	Department of Immigration Inspector.
EVY	A prostitute involved with Hopkinson.
SOPHIE	A prostitute involved with Georg.
GEORG	A German national.
A WOMAN	A Sikh immigrant, British subject.

THE SCENE -- A brothel, Vancouver, 1914

PRODUCTION NOTE
It is important that the scenes flow together without blackouts and without regard to time and setting. The brothel is the major playing area. Surrounding it is an arc or runway used by T.S. and HOPKINSON for most of their scenes. Although T.S. cannot intrude upon the WOMAN's space, he is free to move anywhere else on the set to observe or speak. As the play progresses, T.S.'s scenes move from the arc into the brothel area.

The characters never leave the stage. When not involved in the action, they sit on benches placed on the extreme Stage Right and Stage Left ends of the arc. The WOMAN is on a level above and behind the area used by the other characters. An open grill-like frame in front of her gives both the impression of a cage, and of the superstructure of a ship. T.S. observes the audience entering. The other characters are frozen on stage; the grill-like frame, with the WOMAN behind it, is concealed by a sheet.

THE KOMAGATA MARU INCIDENT

The houselights fade out and a faint light comes up on T.S. who moves to a stool set in the centre of the arc. On this stool are his gloves, hat, and cane. He carefully puts on the gloves while surveying the audience.

T.S.   Good...goood. *(pausing for a moment)* Do you like the suit?

T.S. puts on his top hat, gives it a tap with the cane, looks toward the lighting booth, and snaps his fingers. A spot comes up on him.

Hurry! Hurry! Hurry! Right this way, ladies and gentlemen! First chance to view the Komagata Maru! At this very moment steaming towards picturesque Vancouver Harbour. Yes sireee! The *Komagata Maru*! A first-class -- let the buyer beware -- Japanese steamer, 329.2 feet in length, 2,926 gross tonnage! Captained by one Yomamoto, remember that name. And Japanese crew, carrying a cargo of coal! And 346 Sikhs, count 'em! Plus 30 East Indians, religious affiliation unknown! Add 'em all together and what do you get? That is correct, sir! Give the man a cigar! Three hundred and seventy-six is the answer! Three hundred and seventy-six Asians, to be precise, and all of them bound for Oh Canada, We stand on guard for thee!

T.S. salutes, holds it for a moment, then lets it drop as he moves into the brothel area.

T.S.   This is Vancouver, ladies and gentlemen, the 21st day of May, nineteen hundred and fourteen... And may I direct your attention to my hat...I place the hat on the table...I pass my hands over the hat...and what do we have inside the hat? A pair of gloves! I give you Inspector William Hopkinson, Head of Intelligence, Department of Immigration!

> T.S. *slaps the gloves into* HOPKINSON'*s hand, looks at him for a second, then continues.*

Ladies and gentlemen, the hand is truly faster than the eye...you see this box...and now you don't...and here it is again *(passing it behind his back)* I open it, it's empty, I close the box *(looking at* EVY, *then placing it in her hands)* May I present *(stepping back)* Miss Evy: Entrepreneur!

> T.S. *bangs his cane, spot out.* EVY *and* HOPKINSON *are lit and animated.*

EVY   What is it?

HOPKINSON   It's a present.

EVY   Don't tell me, silly.

HOPKINSON   You asked.

EVY   But I don't want you to tell me.

> HOPKINSON *removes his hand from her eyes.*

EVY   Oh, Bill *(opening the box which contains a brooch)* It's beautiful. Here, pin it on me.

> HOPKINSON *bends over her to do so.* T.S. *bangs his cane, they freeze, spot on* T.S.

T.S.

Ladies and gentlemen! Your attention, please! Now the pocket's empty. Not so now. *(taking out billfold and visa)* I have here one billfold and one German visa for one Georg Braun! *(throwing it on the floor by GEORG)* And here! Behind an ear, a chocolate! *(placing it in SOPHIE's hand)* Allow me to introduce, one Georg Braun and Sophie!

> T.S. *bangs his cane, spot out.* SOPHIE *goes to eat the chocolate,* GEORG *attempts to embrace her, and she pushes him off.*

SOPHIE

Not so fast.

GEORG

Eh?

SOPHIE

No tickee, no washee.

GEORG

I...?

SOPHIE

(putting her hand out) Mon-ey.

GEORG

Oh. *(feeling for his billfold and finding it on the floor as* T.S. *knocks)*

SOPHIE

Somebody get the door! *(plucking billfold from GEORG's hand)* Thank you.

> GEORG *amorously tries to embrace* SOPHIE *again as she counts the money.* T.S. *knocks.* SOPHIE *pushes* GEORG *away.*

SOPHIE

Wait a minute! Are you deaf? There's someone at the door.

> SOPHIE *moves off SR with the billfold. After a moment of indecision, his billfold gone,* GEORG *moves after her.*

GEORG   Ah -- Sophie?

T.S   *(laughing, spot on him)* Ladies and gentlemen.
                   Lest we forget. The *Komagata Maru*. A Japanese
                   steamer chock-full of brown-skin Hindus headed
                   for a predominantly pale Vancouver, and entry
                   into whitish Canada. The *Komagata Maru* in
                   blue Canadian waters!

                         T.S. pulls cover to reveal WOMAN
                         who bends over child on deck. T.S.
                         bows. Spot is out.

WOMAN   Go to sleep. Go to sleep. Shut your eyes, go to
                   sleep.

                         It's very hot and WOMAN turns from
                         the child, wipes her forehead and looks
                         out with a sigh, then turns back to the
                         child.

WOMAN   Still not asleep?

HOPKINSON   *(pinning brooch on)* There. Everything 's
                   forgotten. All right?

EVY   All right.

HOPKINSON   But you have to thank me for the brooch.

EVY   Thank you, Billy.

HOPKINSON   Don't tease. You know I don't like Billy.

EVY   Thank you, Bill.

HOPKINSON   That's better.

EVY   Now you sit down, and I'll get you a drink.

                         HOPKINSON *checks his watch.*

EVY   Oh -- not the time again? You just got here.

HOPKINSON	Can't be helped. I'm sorry.
EVY	You always have to go.
HOPKINSON	Don't be mad. I won't be long, it's just an appointment.
EVY	Bill?
	Still holding the billfold, SOPHIE *crosses round to SL with* GEORG *following.*
SOPHIE	You may as well get used to it. That's what it's like around here. Half the time I'm running messages for him.
GEORG	For who?
SOPHIE	Mr. Hopkinson. Evy's friend with Immigration.
GEORG	Immigration?
SOPHIE	I'm sick of answering that damn door for him.
GEORG	Sophie, do you think--?
SOPHIE	*(at "door" SL)* There's a man out back for Mr. Hopkinson!
HOPKINSON	*(from inside "room")* Who is it?
SOPHIE	He says tell Mr. Hopkinson that Bella Singh is here.
EVY	Your rat again.
HOPKINSON	*(preparing to leave)* Don't call him that.
EVY	I don't like rats coming round.
HOPKINSON	Let's not start this again.

EVY	He's always coming round and when he does, off you go, poof!
HOPKINSON	It'll only take a minute.
EVY	My mother always said, don't snitch, and don't play with snitchers. Didn't your mother ever tell you that?
HOPKINSON	Evy, we've settled all this.
SOPHIE	Mr. Hopkinson! Did you hear me!
HOPKINSON	Now don't pout, you'll get wrinkles.
EVY	Oh, get out.
HOPKINSON	I'm going. *(going to "door")*
SOPHIE	Come on, Georg.
GEORG	Mr. Hopkinson?
HOPKINSON	Who's this, Sophie?
GEORG	Georg Braun, sir, if I could --
WOMAN	See the birds? Land must be near...Mountains, trees, then the island, through the pass. Your uncle will meet us...Look! Soon we will enter the harbour. See where your uncle lives? That is where we'll live.
GEORG	Thank you, sir.
SOPHIE	Georg!

> GEORG *goes to the bench.*
> HOPKINSON *turns back into the room.*

HOPKINSON	Evy? That fellow with Sophie.
EVY	Georg Braun?

HOPKINSON	I've, ah, asked him in for a drink when I get back.
EVY	Oh?
HOPKINSON	I want to meet him.
EVY	You've already met him.
HOPKINSON	Talk to him, then.
EVY	I thought brown rats were your specialty.
HOPKINSON	Bella Singh's a loyal British subject.
EVY	Well, Georg Braun's no British subject! You're setting up no rats in my house!
HOPKINSON	I'll do just as I please in your house! It's me that keeps you open, and don't you forget it! A nod from me, and you'd be buried under warrants. Oh Evy, Evy, Evy...what's good for me is good for you, eh?...Eh Evy? All I want to do is meet him, get to know him better...

> EVY *makes a murmur of protest.*

HOPKINSON	I get ahead, Evy, do you know how I do that? I look ahead, I'm always thinking. Now, you read the papers, you stop and think...With Kaiser Wilhelm and all, something in here tells me a German can do me some good. Eh? Perhaps not today or tomorrow, maybe next year, who knows. Now you can understand that, can't you?
EVY	I just don't like --
SOPHIE	Bella Singh's at the end of the yard! He wants to see you!
HOPKINSON	The German's coming in for a drink, Evy. *(exiting)*

EVY	If -- if you say so.
T.S.	Hopkinson!

        HOPKINSON joins T.S,. DSR arc.

HOPKINSON	Yes sir.
T.S.	The *Komagata Maru's* in port with three hundred and seventy-six potential immigrants.
HOPKINSON	Yes sir.
T.S.	So? What do you know about them?
HOPKINSON	I've spoken to my man, Bella Singh, sir. He tells me they're Sikhs from India, British subjects, and as such they do have right of entry to Canada, sir.
T.S.	The word is no entry.
HOPKINSON	I realize that, but we may have a problem.
T.S.	A what?
HOPKINSON	Many are veterans of the British Army, sir; they're sure to plead consideration for military service.
T.S.	You can put it this way -- we don't mind them dying for us, we just don't want them living with us. *(laughing)* Get the point?
HOPKINSON	*(laughing)* Yes sir...but if they should go to the courts --
T.S.	They won't go to the courts. He hasn't done his homework. Have you forgotten our two orders-in-council? If an immigrant wishes to enter the country through a western port, he must make a continuous voyage from his own country to here. Have they done so?

HOPKINSON   No sir, they haven't.

T.S.   And that's no surprise. There's not a steamship line in existence with a direct India-to-China route and for our second ace-in-the-hole -- a tax, two hundred dollars per head, to be paid before entry. Do they have it?

HOPKINSON   Bella Singh says they do not, however --

T.S.   Again, not surprising. In the land of his birth, the average Indian's wage is nine dollars per year. There -- you see how we operate, Hopkinson? Never a mention of race, colour, or creed -- and yet, we allow British subjects; we don't allow them to enter.

HOPKINSON   Thank you, sir. However, I must inform you that Hermann Singh says --

T.S.   Sh, sh.

HOPKINSON   *(lowering his voice)* Hermann Singh says that the local Sikhs have raised the money for the head tax.

T.S.   That's not so good.

HOPKINSON   It's possible that a launch --

T.S.   It is possible? Do you pay for information like that?

HOPKINSON   Bella Singh says a launch will deliver the head tax to those on the ship late tonight.

T.S.   The word is no entry, Hopkinson.

HOPKINSON   Yes sir.

SOPHIE *rushes into the room followed by* GEORG.

SOPHIE	Listen everybody! Here it is! *(reading from paper)* "Immigration Officials Intercept Head Tax in Vancouver Harbour."

> EVY *enters SR.* HOPKINSON *enters from arc.*

WOMAN	Look! A launch is coming! Maybe it's your uncle.
SOPHIE	There's your name right there! Inspector William Hopkinson.
WOMAN	Be careful! You'll fall!
SOPHIE	Look, Georg! Look, Evy!
WOMAN	The Immigration boat is stopping the launch.
SOPHIE	There it is again, "Hopkinson declares -- "
WOMAN	Shhhhhh. Don't be afraid.
SOPHIE	You read it, Evy, what's it say?
HOPKINSON	I can tell you what it means. British Columbia wants no Calcutta coolies. We've Chinamen and Japs running our shops, Greeks running our hotels, Jews running our second-hand stores, and we don't want Hindus running our mills.
EVY	For God's sake, Bill, have a drink.
T.S.	Have a drink.
HOPKINSON	*(offering bottle)* Georg?
GEORG	Please. The Sikhs on the ship would pay the head tax with the money from the launch, eh? And what is legal? Can you intercept it like that?
HOPKINSON	Well, we did. Another bottle, Evy. The Calcutta coolie, Georg, belongs in India.

GEORG   Do you know India, sir?

HOPKINSON   Do I know India? He wants to know if I know India, Evy.

EVY   Does he know India!

                    EVY *gives him a bottle, sits at the table and begins to play cards.*

HOPKINSON   I know India, and I know its people. When I was a child, my father was stationed in the Punjab -- He had only to shout "Quai Hai" to summon a slave -- a servant -- no, goddamn it, a slave, to summon a slave, to scrawl his initials on a chit, and there was a felt carpet from Kashmir, brass orrnaments from Moradabad, silver for pocket money, cigars, a horse, a dog, anything he wanted. Show him your brooch, Evy. It belonged to my father. Wonderful craftsmen, the natives.

GEORG   It's lovely.

HOPKINSON   Did you know "loot" was an Indian word?

GEORG   Is it?

SOPHIE   *(examining the brooch)* Really beautiful.

HOPKINSON   My father was a big man, blond curly hair, wonderful moustache he had, looked like a prince in his uniform. A prince -- surrounded by little beige people. *(laughing)*

SOPHIE   What about your mother?

HOPKINSON   "Quai Hai!" That's all, and they'd scuttle like bugs.

SOPHIE   Did your mother like it there?

HOPKINSON   She never said. You've no idea, Georg, of the
              size, the immensity, and the millions. *(smiling)*
              When I was a boy I used to like to read at night,
              alone, in a room that had dimensions.

GEORG   Sophie tells me you yourself served in the
              Punjab.

HOPKINSON   Oh, yes. Lahore Police Force. Six years service.

GEORG   And how do you end up in Canada, sir?

HOPKINSON   Promotion was blocked in Lahore.

GEORG   That's hard to believe for a man like...yourself.

HOPKINSON   Quite simple, Georg. Cliques. And I learnt
              something from that. So. I answered an ad and
              here I am.

GEORG   Your life has been very exciting --

SOPHIE   Sophie can make your life exciting too, yes, she
              can. Let Sophie sit on Georg!

              > SOPHIE *lifts her skirts and plunks
              > herself on him. They both fall over on
              > the floor as* T.S. *bangs his cane. They
              > freeze.*

T.S.   Ladies and gentlemen! The turbaned tide is
              flowing! May 23rd, 1914. The first wave of an
              Asian Invasion sits at anchor in Vancouver
              Harbour!

WOMAN   They won't let us land! I've told you. We've
              asked a judge to rule on the orders-in-council.
              Now go!...Our food and our water are rationed.
              How long must we wait?

T.S.   Today's lesson is taken from the Department of Immigration's handbook, Regulation 23, Paragraph 4. I am talking about Checks and Balances of Power. Now, I am the Department of Immigration, I have the power to hold proceedings, make decisions, give orders. I can detain and deport any person or potential immigrant on any grounds whatsoever, unless that person is a Canadian citizen. You are the courts. You have the power to review, reverse, and restrain, quash, and otherwise interfere with my power to hold, to make, and to give, to detain and deport. And you do. Fairly often. It's annoying. So what do I do? Quite simple. I pass Catch 22, Regulation 23, Paragraph 4, which states: "No judge and no court and no officer thereof shall have any jurisdiction to review, reverse, and restrain, quash or otherwise interfere with my holding and making and giving, detaining, deporting."

We are gathered here in the sight of God, and in the spirit of the British Empire to rule on the *Komagata Maru's* contention that Catch 22 Regulation 23, Paragraph 4 is invalid. They maintain that the Department of Immigration has not the authority to deny immigrants access to the courts. If we give them access, then a judge or a court or an officer thereof could overthrow our orders-in-council of which we have two denying them entry -- And that, my good friends, would open the floodgates!

> T.S. *bangs his cane.* GEORG *picks himself up in embarrassment, pushing* SOPHIE *aside.*

GEORG   My...my feelings are this, sir. If you examine the world and its history, you will see that the laws of evolution that have shaped the energy, enterprise, and efficiency of the race northwards have left less richly endowed the peoples inhabiting the southern regions.

HOPKINSON	Go on.
GEORG	Yes. This...this process is no passing accident, but part of the cosmic order of things which we have no power to alter. The European races must administrate; all that's needed to assure their success is a clearly defined conception of moral necessity. Do you agree, sir?
HOPKINSON	Agreed. It's a pleasure to talk to you, Georg. I feel as if you're a friend, a good friend.
GEORG	I'm honoured.
HOPKINSON	I have very few friends. A man in my position, Head of Intelligence, has very few friends.
GEORG	Please consider me one of them.
HOPKINSON	I'm thought of most often as a dose of salts; not palatable, but essential for the health of the body. I accept this.
GEORG	You are --
HOPKINSON	But! If I may make a small observation? It's truly amazing the number of people who use laxatives regularly, and lie about it. Eh? *(laughing)* You follow me, eh?

> HOPKINSON *laughs and* GEORG *joins in.*

HOPKINSON	Yes, I have my job, and I do it. And damn well, if I say so myself.
GEORG	You've a good network of men.
HOPKINSON	Uh uh, more than that. It's a sense of responsibility, that's what it is. I take the risks, and I find my reward in the fulfillment of my task. Now there's your difference between white and coloured -- the Gift of Responsibility.

EVY   *(looking up from her cards)* What's the difference?

HOPKINSON   You see that's why we're sitting in here, and the *Komagata Maru's* out there scratching at the door.

EVY   Why?

HOPKINSON   For Christ's sake, Evy, if it weren't for the British, they couldn't construct a canoe, must less charter a steamer.

EVY   *(back to her cards)* You should know, I suppose. You lived with them.

HOPKINSON   I did not live with them!

EVY   Well, you were there God knows I've heard it often enough. It's hard to keep straight where you were when and with who.

HOPKINSON   I was brought up in India! I know them, if that's what you mean. Keep your mouth shut when we're talking! *(picking up bottle and starting off)* Come on, Georg, I've a chess set, hand-carved from ivory. *(moving off with GEORG following)* Marvellous chess player, my father.

WOMAN   I saw what you did! Do you think because I have no man you can steal food from my child? If you steal again, I will come when you sleep and I'll kill you!

T.S.   *(DSR, arc)* Ah, Hopkinson.

HOPKINSON   I have observed suffering and deprivation on the *Komagata Maru.*

WOMAN   The child cries! He is thirsty!

T.S.   What else?

HOPKINSON	Our policy of disallowing the supplying of the ship is sound. It weakens their morale. It's only a matter of time till they question their leadership...
T.S.	Continue.
HOPKINSON	As...conditions deteriorate, we could, at some future date, offer supplies as an incentive to leave.
T.S.	Very good. Very good.
HOPKINSON	There is...a woman and child on the ship.
T.S.	Irrelevant.
WOMAN	It's hard to explain to a child...Your father was a soldier, he died fighting for the king, so we come to live with your uncle. But first -- we must wait...
SOPHIE	My feet hurt.
EVY	Mmn?
SOPHIE	I don't know why. I'd have thought it'd be my back.

EVY *looks at* SOPHIE *and laughs.*

SOPHIE	What?*(laughing)* Noo. Back trouble runs in the family.
EVY	Oh.
SOPHIE	In the women, that is. With the men it's always having to, you know, piss when they're older.

EVY *laughs.*

SOPHIE	Yeah, I guess if I had my druthers, I'd rather have a bad back...In the night when the pot was full, Grampa would piss out the window...Unless the wind blew from the east. Then he pissed out the door.
EVY	Why?
SOPHIE	It blew back at the window. The window faced east.
EVY	Oh Sophie.

They both laugh.

SOPHIE	It's true...I used to lie on my back in the field and Mama would scream "Sophie, Sophie!" and I'd lie there and think, "Sophie, get out of here, better yourself!"...And Mama would scream "Sophie ! I know you're hidin' "...and I'd just lie there...Mama always said I was lazy. Maybe I am, but you don't see me emptying piss pots. I got out of there.
EVY	Don't stop here, Sophie.
SOPHIE	My back's not breaking from too many kids and carrying milk cans. *(looking at her foot)*
EVY	*(as she exits)* Find a nice man, and move on.
SOPHIE	Maybe I sprained it.

> WOMAN *bends over, retching, dry spasms. When she's finished she draws in several deep breaths. She attempts a smile for the child.*

WOMAN	Don't worry...smile, it's only the water. Don't worry. You are a very brave boy. Your uncle will like you. Come, we'll sit on the side where there's shade.

T.S.   I don't understand.

HOPKINSON   I've promised them food and water.

T.S.   Really?

HOPKINSON   I've given my word.

T.S.   And what did you hope to gain from that?

HOPKINSON   Sir --

T.S.   Surely not plaudits from me.

HOPKINSON   Sir, when I boarded the ship for inspection, they
                seized me and were ready to take off in our launch
                and head for shore, patrol boats or not. They were
                desperate. They say they'd rather be shot than die
                of hunger and thirst. I felt it only -- humanitarian
                to grant one week's provision.

T.S.   You've enabled them to hang on. That's what
                you've done!

HOPKINSON   I saw the mother and child --

T.S.   Now where's that incentive to leave?

HOPKINSON   Their case is still pending.

T.S.   Never initiate action when you haven't the guts
                to carry it through. It's a sign of weakness,
                Hopkinson.

HOPKINSON   Yes sir.

T.S   You disappoint us.

HOPKINSON   Yes sir.

T.S.   We brought you up. We can put you down.

HOPKINSON   Yes sir.

T.S.   We trust that our meaning's sufficiently clear?

HOPKINSON   Yes sir.

                    EVY *enters the room SL.*

EVY   Bill!

SOPHIE   Evy!

EVY   Bill!

SOPHIE   Mr. Hopkinson!

                    HOPKINSON *enters SR.*

HOPKINSON   What's the matter?

EVY   Oh, Bill.

SOPHIE   I thought you went shopping.

EVY   I just -- sat on the tram. A round trip. I never got off it.

HOPKINSON   Come on, Evy.

SOPHIE   Are you sick?

EVY   I...was on the tram. I had a seat by the window. When we...

HOPKINSON   Come on now.

EVY   When we came round by the creek there was a queue for employment, a long line of men looking for work. They were standing in line, we'd stopped for a fare, and then...the line...all of a sudden it... there was a man in a turban at the end of the line, his eye had caught my eye as I looked out the window -- he looked so -- solid -- and I smiled...and he smiled...and as he smiled a man stepped in front of him, and he was back at

EVY *(continued)* the end...Then, I don't know, it happened so quickly, he touched the man on the shoulder, the man turned...and the long line of men, it seemed to turn. The man in the turban started to speak, he got out a few words, I didn't sense anger -- and then it exploded. They knocked him down, the man in the turban they were kicking, and then pushing and shoving to get in a blow -- and the tram pulled away...it was gone. As if I'd imagined it. It had never been.

HOPKINSON You were frightened, that's all.

EVY I should have done something.

HOPKINSON You should have come home and you did. Come on now, you saw a fight. You've seen fights before.

EVY No, it wasn't a fight! And I just sat on the goddamn tram and came home.

HOPKINSON *(to* SOPHIE*)* Get her a drink.

> EVY *goes to look out the window, at the audience, where the Komagata Maru sits.*

EVY There are...people at the end of Burrard, staring out at that ship...They look like the men in that line.

HOPKINSON That's why we're sending the *Komagata Maru* back, so things like your fight won't happen. We don't want them here.

> SOPHIE *exits after giving him drink.*

EVY But why does it happen?

HOPKINSON All I know, Evy, is my father didn't die in the service for the world to be overrun by a second-rate people.

EVY   You don't make sense. Who's second-rate when you run out of brown people?

HOPKINSON   Drink your drink.

EVY   I don't want a drink! *(speaking while exiting SR)* You belong on Burrard.

HOPKINSON follows her.

HOPKINSON   Evy!

T.S   Mr. Speaker; Prime Minister; Honourable Members. Today I am opening my heart to you. I am telling you my fears -- fears that affect each and every Canadian today...I fear for my country, and I fear for my people...I am not ashamed, nor should you be, to state that this is white man's country! And I can tell you that our British legacy, our traditions, those things that we hold dear, that we have fought and died for, is placed in jeopardy today by a massive influx of coloured foreigners! The class of East Indian that has invaded British Columbia is commonly known as Sikh -- having been accustomed to the conditions of a tropical clime, he is totally unsuited to this country. He is criminally inclined, unsanitary by habit, and roguish by instinct. The less we speak of his religion, the better. Suffice it to say that unless his ridiculous forms of worship are relinquished, he is an affront to a Christian community. His intelligence is roughly that of our Aborigines. He indeed belongs to a heathen and debased class. Honourable Members, stand up and be counted! Admit the honest fears of your constituents! Will the Sikh work for cheaper wages. and thus take away their jobs? Will he bring out his women, children, relatives and friends. Will Canadians step on a tram next week to ride from home to work and never hear a word of English spoken?

T.S.   *(continued)* And once at work, if they still have a job, who will they eat their lunch with? Men, honest and true like ourselves, whose fathers made this country what it is today -- or will they be surrounded by coloured men with foreign food? Canadians have rights! Our fathers died for them! Let any man who is not willing to do the same step down! I've told you here today what's in my heart. For God's sake, show me what's in yours!

HOPKINSON *enters SL.*

HOPKINSON   Evy!

EVY *enters SR.*

EVY   I'm here.

HOPKINSON   Was Bella Singh around?

EVY   Don't ask me.

HOPKINSON   Where's Sophie? Sophie!

SOPHIE *enters SR.*

SOPHIE   What?

HOPKINSON   Was Bella Singh around?

SOPHIE   When?

HOPKINSON   Day before yesterday, goddamn it, was he here?

SOPHIE   Maybe. I don't remember.

HOPKINSON   What the hell do you mean, you don't remember?

EVY   Look, Bill, my girls don't keep track of your rats.

HOPKINSON	If they don't, they better start. Customs picked up three men at the border today. Sikhs smuggling guns for the *Komagata Maru*. And my head's on the block! That's the kind of information I'm paid to deliver! And I knew nothing. Do you hear that? Sweet bugger all! Was Bella Singh around or not?
EVY	You can leave now, Sophie.
HOPKINSON	She'll leave when I tell her. Did you forget a message, Sophie?
EVY	You run your business, I'll run mine; Sophie, get out!
HOPKINSON	*(grabbing* SOPHIE*)* By Jesus, I want an answer!
EVY	Me! It was me! Bella Singh came round, he left a note, I threw it out!
	HOPKINSON *releases* SOPHIE. *She leaves.*
HOPKINSON	Why did you do that?
EVY	I don't pass notes.
HOPKINSON	It's me they come down on. Don't you realize that? If I don't deliver, I'm the one that pays -- not Bella Singh. Why did you do it?
EVY	I'm sorry.
HOPKINSON	No you're not.
EVY	No, I'm not.
HOPKINSON	You wanted to make me look bad, is that it?
EVY	No.

HOPKINSON   I look bad enough then they'll dump me. Is that
              what you want?

EVY   No.

HOPKINSON   And off we go! Something else, somewhere else,
              eh?

EVY   What's wrong with that? People do it!

HOPKINSON: Not me.

EVY   Don't you like honest work?

HOPKINSON   That's a funny remark from a whore!

EVY   You want to know why I threw out your note?
              I'll tell you why! I'm a whore and what you do is
              offensive to me! What you do would gag me! I'm
              a whore and when I look at your job, I could
              vomit!

              HOPKINSON *slaps her.*

WOMAN   Don't look at the crowd on the shore!...don't
              listen, pretend they aren't there...the sky is a
              blue, a beautiful blue...look at it! Don't look at
              them on the shore, they are ugly!

              WOMAN *turns her back and begins to
              sing to the child.*

HOPKINSON   I never think of the woman and child they never
              enter my mind...Mewa Singh is a mill worker
              and priest caught crossing the border with guns.
              Mewa Singh is a trusted man in the Sikh
              community. Mewa Singh is a man I could use...I
              speak to him in his jail cell. I begin with
              loyalty, move on to money, end up with threats.
              Mewa Singh says nothing. He looks me straight
              in the eye. I don't always like that, with some
              it's an act of defiance...

HOPKINSON   *(continued)* In Mewa Singh's eyes there is an
infinite sadness, and surrounding him is a pool of
silence, and as I speak and the words fall on my
ears as if from a distance...I think of an incident
when I was a child...there was trouble at the
bazaar...the soldiers had to come in on their
horses...and the next day I walked through...I saw
blood, like clots of dark jelly still on the
streets...but no people...an empty bazaar. Do you
have any conception of how strange that is? I
remember standing very still, scrawny and pasty,
very still, afraid to move...in the middle of
silence, listening, like a mouse on a pan,
listening, for the beat of the wings of the
owl...very still...And then as I stood there, I saw
a figure approaching from one of the streets.
Some native person. He stopped in the shadow of
the huts...he extended his arms towards me...and
I...turned around...and ran home. I was
frightened...Mewa Singh...when I finish my
mixed bag of offers Mewa Singh turns his head
towards the window. It's narrow and barred. He
has dismissed me. His answer is no. Goddamn it!
I need a man who they trust! I'm the one who has
something to lose!

T.S.   Relax! Don't worry! Congratulations are in
order...The courts have come through! Catch 22,
Regulation 23, Paragraph 4 still stands!

> *Carnival music, the air of a party.*
> SOPHIE, GEORG, *and* EVY *join*
> HOPKINSON *on stage.*

T.S.   Hurry! Hurry! Hurry! Final Immigration ruling
on the *Komagata Maru*! Right this way, folks!
Right this way! July 16th, 1914! Last and final
chance to view the *Komagata Maru*! Anchored in
picturesque Vancouver Harbour these last six
weeks and two days! Yes sireeee! A decision is
made!

T.S. *(continued)* Of three hundred and seventy-six Asians, twenty individuals have proven to Immigration Officials the legality of their Canadian domicile; ninety suffering from disease are ordered deported and the rest can just shove off! The Immigration Department reigns supreme! To hell with the judges, the courts and the officers thereof! Last chance to view! The *Komagata Maru*! Take it away, Bill!

Everyone's been drinking and it shows.

HOPKINSON Fare thee well, *Komagata Maru*! Have a pleasant journey!

GEORG Fare thee well!

HOPKINSON Bon voyage! You had your day in court --

SOPHIE Goodbye you Hindus!

HOPKINSON Now you and yours can eat crow from here to Calcutta! Crow with seagull, crow with seaweed, or crow with seawater!

SOPHIE *(laughing)* Crow!

HOPKINSON Fare thee well! Fare thee well!

They're all roaring with laughter, except EVY.

HOPKINSON Fare thee well *Komagata Maru*!

EVY Is it moving yet?

HOPKINSON Not yet, but any minute.

SOPHIE That's funny.

HOPKINSON Have a drink, Evy.

SOPHIE	That's very funny. Why would they want to eat crow with seawater?
GEORG	Who knows what Hindus eat?

GEORG *and* SOPHIE *are laughing still.*

SOPHIE	Still, crow and seawater? It would make you sick. It would make me sick.
GEORG	You aren't a Hindu.
SOPHIE	It'd make anybody sick!
GEORG	Silly, silly, Sophie.
HOPKINSON	See, Evy? It's all over.
SOPHIE	You wouldn't eat that unless you had nothing else to eat, that's for sure.
GEORG	Silly, silly.
SOPHIE	Hey, crow and seawater sounds awful too.
HOPKINSON	Forget it, Sophie.
SOPHIE	Eh?
HOPKINSON	It's just an expression.
SOPHIE	So what's it mean?
HOPKINSON	Come on, Evy.
SOPHIE	*(louder)* Eh?
HOPKINSON	To submit humbly!
EVY	Surely that rings a bell, I mean, it does for me.
SOPHIE	What?

HOPKINSON	Don't be like that. Say you're sorry. I'm sorry.
SOPHIE	Come on, Georg.

> GEORG *embraces* SOPHIE.

SOPHIE	Where's the music -- you gotta have music for a party!
HOPKINSON	Sophie's right.
GEORG	What we'll have is a polka!

> GEORG *and* SOPHIE *wind up the gramophone.*

HOPKINSON	It's a party! Come on, Evy, let's dance.
SOPHIE	I love to polka! It's hard on the feet, but I love it!

> *They dance to the music.*

T.S.	Hopkinson!

> HOPKINSON *stops dancing.*

T.S.	There's someone at the end of the yard. Bella Singh's at the end of the yard!

> HOPKINSON *exits* EVY *follows him for a step or two, then stops.* SOPHIE *and* GEORG *dance, carry the bottle and laugh.*

WOMAN	We hear them rejoice on the shore...They say we are beasts; physical death is no evil for us, it may be a blessing, else why pestilence and famine? They say we are the enemies of Christ, the Prince of Peace; they will hate us with a perfect hatred; they will blast us with grape shot and rockets; they will beat us as small as dust before the wind!

The music stops. SOPHIE *and* GEORG
collapse.

WOMAN	They say our appeal to the courts is dismissed. They say tonight the *Komagata Maru* will sail for India.
T.S.	*(winking)* Guess again!
HOPKINSON	The bastards!
WOMAN	On the ship a meeting is held. I vote in the place of my son who is five. It is right that we're here!
HOPKINSON	*(gazing out at the ship)* Sit tight in the harbour, will they?
EVY	Drink up, everyone.
HOPKINSON	The foolish bastards. They must think it's a cricket game with the officers. Fair play. Your wicket. Pass the crumpets.
GEORG	So what can they do?
HOPKINSON	Bugger all. A move can't be made nor a word whispered, on the street, in the temple, on the waterfront, without my knowing it.
EVY	He has his men! His men produce! Eh, Bill?
HOPKINSON	If they don't, they'll find themselves in steerage on the next ship out!
EVY	*(drunk)* You know something?
HOPKINSON	I'll seal the *Komagata Maru* off tighter than paint on a wall.
EVY	You sound worried.

HOPKINSON	I'll see it wrapped round with rot and rust and manned by skeletons before one bastard disembarks!
EVY	Come on, everyone! It's a party!
HOPKINSON	That's right! Glasses up, glasses up! Here's to the *Komagata Maru* -- stuck in picturesque Vancouver Harbour! It gives me great pleasure to extend to you the hospitality of the Canadian people! Enjoy your anchorage! Sip our rain and eat our air! And when you've had your fill -- India lies westward!
T.S.	Ladies and gentlemen! It walks! It talks! It reproduces! It provides cheap labour for your factories, and a market for your goods! All this, plus a handy scapegoat! Who's responsible for unemployment! The coloured immigrant! Who brings about a drop in take-home pay? The coloured immigrant! Who is it creates slum housing, racial tension, high interest rates, and violence in our streets? The coloured immigrant! Can we afford to be without it? I say "No!" It makes good sense to keep a few around -- when the dogs begin to bay, throw them a coloured immigrant! It may sound simple, but it works. Remember though -- the operative word's "a few" -- For reference, see the Red, the White, the Blue and Green Paper on Immigration, whatever year you fancy!
EVY	*(still drinking)* This place is a pigsty.
SOPHIE	That's old news, Evy.
EVY	This place is a pigsty.
SOPHIE	At least it's a profitable pigsty -- isn't it?
EVY	Money isn't everything. *(laughing as no one else reacts)*...eh?

SOPHIE   Don't be silly.

EVY   Did you know that if a pig falls in a trough, the other pigs would eat him. *(playing cards)* Gobble, gobble gobble...I think pigs are all right...I've known some not bad pigs...it's the goddamn pigstys that turn them nasty...

GEORG   *(sitting reading a German paper)* I would not want to be Kaiser Wilhelm today...

EVY   Why? Isn't he feeling well. *(laughing as no one else reacts)* Oh well...that's too bad...maybe tomorrow?...

SOPHIE   It's so hot. At home you always get a breeze off the water.

EVY   In Manitoba you don't.

GEORG   *(turning page)* If war should break out...well...

EVY   *(brightly)* People will die, eh ?

> EVY *looks at* HOPKINSON *who stands staring out at the ship.*

EVY   Bill?...Bill, a watched pot never boils.

T.S.   *(speaking very quietly, his stance mirroring* HOPKINSON's*)* What we need is a reason to board her. To mount a police action, preliminary, whatever. To arrest those aboard.

EVY   Leave the window alone, Bill.

T.S   We could board them, arrest them, escort them to the open sea, and once there, release them, pointed towards India.

EVY   Come talk to me.

T.S.	Now if the captain and crew charged the Sikhs with mutiny, we'd be away, eh?
EVY	Bill?
T.S.	The captain refuses to press charges? Really? You know, I can't help but feel you don't give full vent to your powers of persuasion. One begins to wonder whose side you're on, someone should check out your file. A good man would find a reason to board her.
HOPKINSON	Yes..
SOPHIE	It's the heat. It's so hot.

SOPHIE *gets up and exits.*

HOPKINSON	It's July...It's supposed to be hot...

T.S. *howls in a boy scout position, on his haunches, two fingers of each hand at his temples.*

T.S.	Akela says "Be Prepared." *(howling)* Akela says "Do your Duty for God and the King, and Obey the Law of the Pack." *(howling, then stop abruptly and rising)* Akela says I have three merit badges for the boy who comes up with a first-rate reason to board the *Komagata Maru*!
EVY	What're you writing?
HOPKINSON	Nothing.
EVY	Are you writing in German, what is it?
HOPKINSON	It's nothing...now...clear off, I'm busy.

EVY *wanders off SL.*

WOMAN	This is not where we live...we shall not see your uncle...but we can't cross an ocean without water or food...You must not be afraid, for hundreds of years the Khyber Pass has run with our blood, we're not afraid to spill more of it here!Do you hear me ashore! We have suffered, but we have endured! We are tempered like steel! We are ready!
HOPKINSON	Georg?
GEORG	Mnn? *(from behind his paper)*
HOPKINSON	I was wondering.
GEORG	Yes?
HOPKINSON	I have a small problem...perhaps you could advise me...
GEORG	Certainly. What is your problem?
HOPKINSON	It's the *Komagata Maru*.
GEORG	*(laughing)* You call this a small problem?
HOPKINSON	*(doesn't like the laugh)* Compared to, say, Kaiser Wilhelm, of course. Compared to that of an enemy alien in this country if war should break out, yes, I think a small problem, don't you?

GEORG *gets the point.*

T.S.	It's not what you call subtle, but it works.
HOPKINSON	I wish to make the *Komagata Maru* an offer -- to give them supplies, to make some vague promise of promises, to recompense them for their cargo of coal, to entice them to sail. I wish the whole transaction kept quiet.
GEORG	And what is your problem?

HOPKINSON   If my offer got out, it might look like some kind of acknowledgement of their rights, and in this affair, they have none.

                      GEORG *goes to speak.*

HOPKINSON   As for Bella Singh and the rest, well, to be blunt, I don't trust them -- trustworthy as they are, have been in the past, will be in the future, I do not totally trust them in this endeavour. A very slight qualm of mistrust.

GEORG   I see.

HOPKINSON   What do you advise, my good friend, Georg?

                      EVY *enters unobserved. She's come in for a bottle but stops to listen.*

GEORG   You're looking for someone to carry your offer out to the ship?

HOPKINSON   That's correct. *(drawing out envelope)* This particular offer -- a man I can trust -- a man for whom I possibly could do a small favour sometime in the future in return for this favour...

GEORG   And with some small financial reward, I suppose?

HOPKINSON   Correct. I will provide a boat, and one of our patrols will study the night sky as you slip through the -- oh -- excuse the use of the pronoun.

GEORG   Quite all right. Quite -- all right -- in fact, is there any reason why I myself, Georg, cannot act on your behalf in this matter?

HOPKINSON   Ah.

GEORG   Shall we drink to it? *(moving to do so)*

HOPKINSON   First the details --

                   They catch sight of EVY.

EVY   Hello.

GEORG   Hello, Evy.

                   HOPKINSON *lowers his voice slightly*
                   as EVY *hovers in background.*

HOPKINSON   First the details, then the drink -- Note, the
                   envelope is sealed, and must remain so.

                   As he passes the envelope to GEORG,
                   EVY *takes it.*

EVY   What's this?

GEORG   *(looking to* HOPKINSON*)* Ah?

EVY   A letter home?

GEORG   Yes. May I have it?

EVY   A letter to Germany -- but it has no address.

HOPKINSON   Give him his letter.

EVY   A letter to Germany -- what is -- someone should
                   open it. What's in it?

HOPKINSON   Evy --

EVY   Georg, where's your head? We're practically at
                   war. The only thing worse than a letter to
                   Germany is a letter from Germany. Governments
                   are paranoid. Ask Bill.

GEORG   Eh?

HOPKINSON   She drinks too much.

EVY   I just had an idea! What if --

HOPKINSON *(making a grab for her arm and missing)* Give it to me!

EVY   I'm not finished! What if a letter containing -- who knows what -- was carried by a German national out to the *Komagata Maru* --

HOPKINSON Shut your mouth.

EVY   -- and intercepted by the Department of Immigration -- what if, eh?

GEORG   What if? *(shrugging)*

EVY   A plot between the Germans and the Sikhs!

GEORG   A plot between...?

> GEORG *laughs with a tinge of nervousness and a look to* HOPKINSON.

GEORG   Give me the letter.

EVY   He wants a good solid reason to board the *Komagata Maru* and by Jesus I'm looking at it!

HOPKINSON You're going to end up in a sailor's bar, Evy.

EVY   I won't let you do this!

HOPKINSON Two-bits-a-crack in a dark alley.

EVY   Georg -- *(giving it to him)* Open it.

GEORG   This is an offer to --

HOPKINSON That's enough.

EVY   It's a trick. Open it!

HOPKINSON	Return it, or deliver it sealed.
GEORG	You don't understand --
HOPKINSON	No trust, no deal.
EVY	Don't you know who he works for?
GEORG	Evy, he works for the government.
EVY	Oh yes!...Oh yes...and I can tell you a story about governments...a bedtime story --
T.S. & EVY	Once upon a time --

The characters freeze as T.S. *moves among them.* T.S. *continues the story.*

T.S.   There was a little boy who came to Manitoba with his mummy and daddy and sisters and brothers and many others very much like him. Their skin was a pale ivory, their eyes a light blue, and their hair dark -- without being too dark -- and curly -- but not too curly! They were running from persecution and injustice...and Canada said: "You wish to own farm land communally? No bother at all! You will not swear allegiance to the crown and the flag? Weeeelllll, what is it, after all, but headgear and a piece of cloth? You do not wish to fight wars? That too can be arranged; exceptions can be made." The daddies worked to earn money for seed and supplies, and the mummies harnessed themselves to the plough and pulled it, breaking the hard brown earth of Manitoba and the soft white flesh of their backs till the red blood ran down, and the little boy walked beside the plough picking bouquets of tiny blue flowers. By and by, the mummies and daddies had homes and barns and food for the winter and seed for the spring and horses for the plough. Then others came and saw what they had.

T.S. *(continued)* And Canada said -- "Now about this allegiance! And which of you owns this particular piece of land? Be precise and sign here! And my goodness, friends, isn't all this worth killing and maiming for? What kind of people are you?" The mummies and daddies and sisters and brothers set out on a pilgrimage. They walked to Yorktown and along the tracks towards Winnipeg.

> T.S. *bangs his cane. The others unfreeze, and* GEORG *turns to* HOPKINSON.

GEORG About this letter! *(extending it)*

EVY Listen to me! I watched them walk past --

> T.S. *bangs his cane. They freeze.*

T.S. It was snowing. They had little to eat, and then nothing to eat, for the Mounties cut off their supplies -- and it snowed. People dropped by the tracks and a special train came along and returned everyone to Northern Manitoba. And those who would not sign and swear allegiance were driven from their land with only what they could carry! *(banging his cane)*

HOPKINSON *(snatching the letter)* I'll make other arrangements!

> T.S. *bangs the cane. They freeze.*

T.S. Then people whose skins were so fair as to be opalescent, whose eyes were so light they shone in the dark, whose hair sparkled like dust motes in the sun, with each strand hanging in a manner that can only be described as poker straight -- these people stormed the land office for homesteads and barns and harvests still in the fields.

EVY   My brother stood in line for three days, he got a section -- next to my father's.

T.S.   And they all lived happily ever after!...There now. Good night, sleep tight, don't let the bedbugs bite...Shhhhhhhhhhh! *(tiptoeing away)*

EVY   It can happen to any of us.

HOPKINSON   Go to bed.

EVY   Look at him. He'd cut off his hand before he'd make the *Komagata Maru* an offer. *(laughing)* He's got a thing about race, about colour, haven't you noticed?

HOPKINSON   You're boring and stupid, Evy.

EVY   Why do you suppose that is?

GEORG   I --

EVY   He goes to the temple.

GEORG   Eh?

EVY   Gets himself all dolled up, goes to the temple in disguise -- he thinks he looks like a Sikh. I bet the Sikhs think he looks like an ass.

HOPKINSON   Good night, Georg.

GEORG   About --

HOPKINSON   Good night.

　　　　　　　　GEORG *gives a little bow and leaves.*

EVY   I've been thinking. Funny thing, your background --

HOPKINSON   That's enough.

EVY	Birthplace, things like that, where were you born, Bill?
HOPKINSON	Get the hell upstairs.
EVY	Where?
HOPKINSON	England.
EVY	Where in England, be specific.
HOPKINSON	Yorkshire!
EVY	Yorkshire? Yorkshire! Now that's a new one, Yorkshire, eh?...That's not what I think.
HOPKINSON	Evy!
EVY	Quick, Georg *(pretending* GEORG *is still there)* without looking, what colour's his eyes, wanna bet? I'd say brown.

> *Sometime during this scene,*
> **HOPKINSON** *begins to subtly stalk*
> *her. She as subtly avoids him.*

HOPKINSON	You filthy bitch!
EVY	Blue, did you say? Well then I bet his mother's eyes were brown.
HOPKINSON	My mother's dead.
EVY	Born in Punjab, served by Yorkshire.
HOPKINSON	Born in Yorkshire!
EVY	So are they blue or brown?
HOPKINSON	Blue!
EVY	Your mother's eyes, now what were they?

HOPKINSON   My mother's eyes were blue, you bitch! I'll kill you.

EVY   First you'll have to catch me.

> HOPKINSON *chases her; she avoids him.*

EVY   You're stupid, Bill, you're stupid...it's not me that's stupid, it's you. Stupid, stupid, Bill.! They all use you, Bill, yes, they do...You think that you use Georg, you think that you use Bella Singh, you think that you use me, but you're the one that's being used...they're using you and Billy Boy's too dumb to know and stupid dumbo Billy will keep on being used cause Billy Dumbo's stupid! Stupid dumbo Billy's stupid dumbo Billy.

> HOPKINSON *catches* EVY; *she speaks softly.*

EVY   And Billy's mother's brown.

> HOPKINSON *slaps* EVY; *she speaks louder.*

EVY   And Billy's mother's brown!

> HOPKINSON *slaps* EVY; *she speaks louder.*

And Billy's mother's brown.

> HOPKINSON *throws* EVY *down, kneels and shakes her.*

HOPKINSON   Don' t say that. Don' t say that! I'll kill you if you say that to me! *(slowing down his attack on her)* Evy, don' t say that. Please don' t say that...*(stopping)* I...I love you, Evy, don't say that to me...

EVY *reaches out and draws his head to her.*

EVY Oh...oh...poor, poor, Billy.

T.S. Hopkinson!

HOPKINSON *moves very slowly and speaks without expression. It's an effort for him to get up.*

T.S. What're you waiting for...where's your report?

HOPKINSON Sir.

T.S. You've come up with what?

HOPKINSON Sir.

T.S. A reason to board her, remember?

HOPKINSON: Sir.

T.S. Kindly observe *(clearing his throat)* Captain Yomamoto! Captain Yomamoto! Is there a Captain Yomamota in the house? Ah, my dear Captain, there you are. If you wouldn't mind taking a seat.

T.S. *indicates a chair for the* CAPTAIN *who is exceedingly short.*

T.S. How many times have we had this conversation? How many times must we have this conversation? Yes, yes, I know what you said before: "strictly speaking" your passengers have not mutinied, hence you are reluctant to lay a charge...Truly a commendable stance -- however. Let us forget "strictly speaking" for a moment. How about trying "laxly speaking," "loosely speaking," "informally speaking" --

T.S.

(continued) -- could you find it in your heart to lay a charge "loosely speaking" against the passengers of the *Komagata Maru*?...Nothing has changed, huh?...Not so quick, Captain, one more minute please...While casually flipping through my classified copy of condensed Canadian law "What to Do in a Pinch" I found the most interesting -- oh, I'm sure you'd be interested -- you see it says right here, as I interpret this small item here...Yes, right here in very small print -- You can't see it? But my dear Captain, I assure you I can. It states: If given formal notice to sail, then sail you must, *toute suite* -- it's a bilingual law -- or be subject to a fine of $500.00 That's per person aboard. "With- the-Power-Vested-in-Me-by-His-Majesty's Government-I-Hereby-Give-You-Formal-Notice-to-Sail.!" Now, let me see, 500 times 356, that's put down the zero, carry the three - what was that you just said? You wish to press charges? Mutiny, sedition, treason, and -- blackmail? Be serious, my dear fellow, the first is sufficient...

Mutiny!

M - that's Militia for instilling fear,
U - Union Jack which God knows we hold dear,
T - for a tugboat, one you can't sink,
I - for informant, a nice word for fink,
N - for our Navy of fine volunteers,
Y- for Yomamoto, who finally signed

Here!
Hopkinson! Here are your papers.
Now, my good man, do your duty.

> GEORG *helps* HOPKINSON *on with his jacket.*

GEORG

I'm sorry about the letter. I pay no attention to her. She's a stupid woman.

HOPKINSON	Yomamoto has signed, pressed charges of mutiny. The militia is lining the dock, they are armed, they wait in reserve...We will engage the *Komagata Maru* at sea!
GEORG	In the harbour, you mean.
HOPKINSON	In the harbour. *(addressing a crowd)* We will mount an attack from the *Sea Lion*, the largest ocean-going tug in the port! Police Chief MacLennan shall lead 120 policemen and 40 special Immigration Officers --
GEORG	May I volunteer my services, sir?
HOPKINSON	In a paramilitary attack on the ship?
GEORG	Will I come under fire, sir?
HOPKINSON	On board the *Komagata Maru* are veteran soldiers.
GEORG	Are they armed?
HOPKINSON	Reliable sources inform me that weapons abound on the ship. They have made clubs from floating driftwood, possibly spears from bamboo poles.
T.S.	He's forgotten the cargo of coal.
HOPKINSON	Force will be met with force. Rifles will be issued before we embark...
T.S.	*(prompting)* I expect every...
HOPKINSON	I expect every man to do his duty. No doubt we will meet with stubborn opposition, but remember, we are a formidable force!
T.S.	In an orderly manner.
WOMAN	They are coming.

T.S.	Board the *Sea Lion*.
WOMAN	*(softly)* Jai Khalsa...
GEORG	It was fair-sized for a tug, but not large enough for a company of men such as we were.
WOMAN	Stand back from the rail.
GEORG	Four reporters came along for the ride. "Hoppy," they cried, "How about a smile for the press!" Mr. Hopkinson smiled.
WOMAN	Get below.
GEORG	It looked like a very big ship and the closer we got --
WOMAN	They have guns.
GEORG	The more quiet we were...silence...The *Sea Lion* rode low in the water...as we looked up we saw them...lining the rails were great turbanned figures...We stared up at them...they stared down at us...then...
T.S.	*(low)* Throw out the grappling hooks.
WOMAN	*(screaming)* Jai Khalsa!!
GEORG	All hell broke loose!
WOMAN	Jai Khalsa!
GEORG	From three hundred odd throats came a yell!
WOMAN	Jai Khalsa!
GEORG	Followed by bricks from the boiler settings, scrap iron and coal!
WOMAN	Hide!

GEORG	Mostly coal!
WOMAN	Hide below!
GEORG	Coal rains around us!
WOMAN	Jai Khalsa!
GEORG	Hopkinson's hit again and again!
WOMAN	Jai Khalsa!
GEORG	They can see the gold braid on his hat!
HOPKINSON	I look for the woman and child.
GEORG	Get down! For God's sake get down!
WOMAN	Jai Khalsa!
HOPKINSON	I stand as straight as I can.
GEORG	Take off your hat and get down! *(raising his gun to fire)*
HOPKINSON	There's no order to fire! Don't fire!

> WOMAN *throws the missile of coal which knocks* HOPKINSON *down.*

WOMAN	Jai Khalsa!

> *A pause with* HOPKINSON *lying on the floor.* EVY *enters slowly with* SOPHIE. *They help* HOPKINSON *to the sofa and press a cloth to his head.*

GEORG	It was a total and humiliating defeat. What else can you expect? It was ridiculous. We go out with rifles and then never use them. The whole thing was poorly conceived. However, compared to the execution of the scheme, the conception was an act of genius!

SOPHIE	What do you mean?
GEORG	It was a stupid thing to do.
EVY	Hold the cloth to your head, Bill. It's cold. It'll help.
HOPKINSON	I'm all right. I just want something to wash with.
SOPHIE	*(laughing)* I don't wonder. He looks like a chimney sweep, doesn't he, Georg?
GEORG	There you sit, a servant in His Majesty's government, battered and bruised by a bunch of Hindus.
HOPKINSON	Get me some water!
SOPHIE	If you yell you can get it yourself.
GEORG	Tell me the point of carrying rifles if nobody uses them?...And there he stood with his hat. The smart thing to do was remove it. No, there he stood. Every time he was hit, they all cheered. The air rang with cheers!
SOPHIE	I just thought of something *(laughing)* ...Mr. Hopkinson, I guess it was you that ate crow, eh?

> SOPHIE *nudges* GEORG who *chuckles after a slight effort to restrain himself.*

SOPHIE	It was him that ate crow!
HOPKINSON	Get out! Get out and leave me alone!

> SOPHIE *and* GEORG *move to exit SL.*

SOPHIE	It was him that ate crow.

> *They're still chuckling.*

GEORG   Sophie.

               They exit. WOMAN *is at a meeting on
               the ship.*

WOMAN   We have gained nothing but time! We've driven
               them off for only a while, what now we must
               press for is food! I say it is better we starve on
               their doorstep than out on the sea!

HOPKINSON   Do you remember when I gave you your brooch?

EYY   Yes.

HOPKINSON   Do you like it?

EVY   Yes, I do.

T.S.   Order! Order!

               HOPKINSON *begins to adjust his
               clothing.*

EVY   Bill -- this time don't go.

T.S.   Order!

EVY   Say to hell with it.

T.S.   Are you assembled?

               EVY *speaks as* HOPKINSON *joins*
               T.S.

EVY   Don't go, Bill.

T.S.   The meeting will come to order...Well now, that
               was a bit of a balls-up yesterday, wasn't it?...

               HOPKINSON *goes to speak.*

T.S.	However, we aren't here to assign guilt, we can do that later. What's the next step, that's the question. Any suggestions, Hopkinson?

HOPKINSON *shakes his head slowly.*

T.S.	I thought not. Well, luckily we have in our midst a man with courage and foresight. He has had refurbished, refitted, and manned a second-class cruiser at Esquimalt, the *Rainbow*, length 300 feet, 3,600 gross tonnage with two six-inch guns and six four-inch guns. A small hand please for Harry Stevens, our federal M.P....I think we can do better than that.

HOPKINSON *claps.*

T.S.	Ah, yes...Mr. Stevens has worked diligently since the arrival of the *Komagata Maru* in our waters. Diligence, perseverance, and patriotism always pay off. Let the *Rainbow* push through the Narrows; let her anchor near enough to the *Komagata Maru* for the sun to glint on her guns. Let our next message be -- we won't necessarily fire on you -- but we will fire on you if necessary! *(turning to leave)*
HOPKINSON	Sir!...My informants in the Sikh community inform me --
T.S.	Informants inform you? *(laughing)*You're being redundant, my boy.
HOPKINSON	My people in the Sikh community tell me that threats have been made. Death threats.
T.S.	You've stirred up a hornet's nest, haven't you? You've opened up Pandora's Box. You've created a maelstrom.
HOPKINSON	I was following orders.

T.S.	Let me tell you something -- there's someone at the end of the yard...
HOPKINSON	Bella Singh?
T.S.	Not Bella Singh...Someone who's not Bella Singh waits at the end of the yard...
EVY	Who is it out there?
HOPKINSON	One of my men, I imagine.
EVY	Why don't you go out?
HOPKINSON	Later, perhaps...Let him wait.
WOMAN	*(laughing)* Do you know something? My son's lips have swollen and burst from the thirst -- they are covered with grease from the engines. My legs are like sticks -- if I smelt a real meal I would vomit -- and you think a few guns will make our knees knock? *(stopping laughing)* Sale Haramazaade! Give us supplies and we'll leave!
HOPKINSON	See the cruiser...it has guns trained on the *Komagata Maru*.
EVY	Will they fire on it?
HOPKINSON	That -- is not my concern.
EVY	Don't you feel anything for them?
HOPKINSON	You wouldn't understand.
EVY	Yes I would. I would try.
HOPKINSON	One has to make decisions. Commitments. To one side or another.
EVY	What side are you on?
HOPKINSON	The winning side.

EVY   Are you winning?

HOPKINSON   This time the *Komagata Maru* will sail.

EVY   Do you think then you'll have won?

HOPKINSON   I'm...tired. Let's go to bed. *(starting off)*

EVY   Not right now.

>   HOPKINSON *stops, turns to look at*
>   EVY.

HOPKINSON   Lie beside me. That's all.

EVY   I don't want to.

HOPKINSON   I don't have to ask! I can order!

>   EVY *looks at him, then picks up her*
>   *cards, begins to lay them out. After a*
>   *moment,* HOPKINSON *leaves.*
>   *Carnival music plays.*

T.S.   Hurry! Hurry! Hurry! Absolutely the last and
             final chance to view the *Komagata Maru*!
             Anchored in picturesque Vancouver Harbour for
             two, count 'em, two glorious months! Note the
             cruiser standing by to the right, see the sun on
             its guns, what a fantastic sight! Ladies and
             gentlemen, can you truly afford to bypass this
             splendid spectacle? Run, my good friends, you
             mustn't walk, you must run! Cotton candy, taffy
             apples, popcorn and balloons! All this and a
             possible plus, the opportunity to view your very
             own navy in action with no threat to you!

>   *Music stops.*

SOPHIE   It's all so exciting...now tell me what are all the
             little boats doing?

GEORG	Some of them are harassing the Sikhs, some of them are supplying the ship -- the government is giving them provisions.
SOPHIE	And what about the cargo of coal -- if there's any left.
GEORG	I hear the government may recompense them. My friends tell me they have promised them everything and will give them nothing. That's called diplomacy, eh Bill?
SOPHIE	Oh look, everybody! Look! There's black smoke coming out of the smokestack...look the *Rainbow's* moving...it's moving in...what's it going to do...I bet it's to shoot, I hope it's going to shoot, it's...Look, Evy! Come look! It's...It's...it's moving -- The *Komagata Maru's* moving -- and the *Rainbow's* going right along side...We won! We won! Didn't we, Georg? Didn't we, Mr. Hopkinson? Aren't you even going to look? It's over and we won!

A bang of the cane and they freeze.

T.S.	Over?...A note, Mr. Hopkinson, from the man at the end of the yard..."When the affairs were past any other remedy, I thought it righteous to draw my sword."

HOPKINSON *looks at the note.*

WOMAN	(*hard, not sentimental*) We go back. My husband is dead. He died in their war. His father is dead. He died when they cut back the famine relief. I am a British subject, and my people's taxes have gone to their King. I am not a possession, a thing. I am myself and I will fight for myself and my son and my people. I am strong.
GEORG	The whole thing has been most educational. I should thank you. I have made many valuable friends and good contacts.

GEORG	*(continued)* I owe it to you, Bill...Can I get you a drink, Sophie, get him a drink.
HOPKINSON	*(stepping out to T.S.)* I have good men in the Indian community...good men...they produce...Bella Singh, Baboo Singh, Hermann Singh, Gunga Ram --
T.S.	Mewa Singh?
HOPKINSON	Not -- Mewa Singh.
T.S.	For God's sake, get on.
HOPKINSON	Their lives are in danger...the community feels that they're traitors, surely they're loyal British subjects, like myself.
T.S.	Hurry up.
HOPKINSON	My own life has been threatened...I ask for --
T.S.	Extra! Extra! Read all about it! War Declared! Recession Recedes! Factories Hum the National Anthem! Send your sons overseas! See all of Europe at federal expense! Check your programme for casting -- the enemy's the Kraut! The Sikh's on our side! Extra! Extra! Read all about it!
GEORG	*(picking up paper)* This can't help but work nicely for me.
HOPKINSON	What?
GEORG	I say the war shall increase my use to your department.
SOPHIE	Isn't he smart, Evy? Georg is going places -- and so is Sophie.
EVY	*(looking up from her cards)* Christ, Sophie, it's a war.

GEORG	It's also a good business deal.

EVY spits on the floor.

GEORG	You should teach her some manners.
SOPHIE	You're jealous.
EVY	Oh Sophie.
SOPHIE	It's true -- you're jealous of me -- Georg's up and doing -- he gets around -- we have a good time. Look at him -- he doesn't do anything since the *Komagata Maru*. And you're just as bad. This place is just like a morgue. Who wants to live in a morgue? I'll leave if I want to -- I can, you know -- I'll leave anytime I want.
HOPKINSON	No you won't.
SOPHIE	Yes I will. Won't I, Georg? Whenever Georg wants.
HOPKINSON	Georg wants what I give him! When I say move, you bloody well move, when I say jump, you say how high. In this stinking world there's two kinds, there's the ruler and the ruled -- and when I see the likes of you, I know where I stand! *(beginning to weaken)* Some people talk, and some people listen, but by God, I act, and if...it weren't for people like me...people like you...would still be down in the slime...I have my...I have my...
T.S.	Bill?
HOPKINSON	I have...
T.S.	Mewa Singh waits at the end of the yard.
HOPKINSON	Yes.

EVY moves to him.

WOMAN	We dock at Budge Budge fourteen miles from Calcutta. We are to be herded aboard trains and returned to the Punjab although many of us have not been there for years. We resist. Police, reinforced by soldiers, open fire. Men who shared their rancid flour with my son are dead. *(threatening)* We will remember them.
T.S.	Order! Order! The court will come to order! Will the Inspector take the stand! Do you swear to tell the truth, the whole truth, and nothing but the truth, as it befits this case, so help you God?
HOPKINSON	I do.
T.S.	Might I ask if you were acquainted with one Hermann Singh?
HOPKINSON	I was.
T.S.	What was his character?
HOPKINSON	He was a quiet, unassuming man, intensely ioyal to his King.
T.S.	What was the nature of your relationship?
HOPKINSON	He rendered assistance to the government in the *Komagata Maru* Incident.
T.S.	Five and one half weeks after the departure of the *Komagata Maru*, one Pirt Warnes was walking along a little used trail on the Kitsilano Indian Reserve. It was quite a pleasant trail...he noticed what at first glance appeared to be a bundle of rags behind a log close to the path. He examined it. It was the badly decomposed body of an East Indian. The turban was wrapped round the ankles. Beside the body lay a leather satchel, an empty brandy flask, and an open straight razor. When he touched the head it came off in his hand. It was Hermann Singh.

T.S. *(continued)* Let me ask you, Inspector, from your intimate knowledge of the Asian mind, would you say the facts as related are consistent with... suicide?

HOPKINSON No, I would not.

T.S. Ah...and if indeed it were murder, can you suggest a possible motive?

HOPKINSON By informing, Hermann Singh had incurred the hatred of his people.

T.S. You may step down.

EVY Why don't we go away?...Why can't we?...Bill?...Bill, talk to me!...I can leave. I can leave. And I will. *(exiting off stage)*

T.S. Six weeks after the departure of the *Komagata Maru*, Arjun Singh shot through the back of the head from behind!

HOPKINSON Arjun Singh is dead.

GEORG *(on the sofa, feet up, reading the paper)* He'll have to get a new stable of fellows, eh?

SOPHIE *(playing cards)* Where would he find them, eh?

GEORG *(laughing)* Good point...where is he going to find them?

T.S. September 5th, 1914...early evening...Bella Singh goes to the temple. Inside the temple, people are singing. They're singing hymns for Arjun Singh, Hermann Singh...Bella Singh takes off his shoes...Bella Singh enters the temple...Bella Singh moves to the back...Bella Singh sits in a corner...Bella Singh takes out a gun...he fires ten shots, scores nine out of ten, seven wounded, two dead. He never speaks till arrested.

GEORG	Do you know what he says, Sophie? He says that he acted in self-defence, he says Bill will verify that...will you testify, Bill?
HOPKINSON	Yes.
T.S.	October 21st, 1914...My God, what a day! Look at that sky...and the leaves all russet and gold...the mountains like sentinels, just a light breeze, the city set like a precious gem on the Pacific...breathe in...breathe out...breathe in...breathe out...
HOPKINSON	I leave the house early. I walk to the court house...It's fall...I feel like a toy man walking through a toy town. Everything's working. My arms and my legs move so well together, there is ...a mechanical precision to everything...I notice the houses seem neater than usual, a certain precision...at the same time, it's slower, things are slower, but very precise...there are no clouds in the sky, and it's blue, a deep blue...there's a slight breeze...the veins in the leaves protrude as if swollen...toy mountains frame my toy town...I'm just a bit late because of the walk. I enter the court house from Howe Street. As I wait for the lift to take me up to the court, I place very carefully one hand on the wall, feeling the wall, and feeling my hand on the wall, in this tiny toy court...I open the door of the lift, I step inside, then I close it. I think of the peace of the coffin. I think of the safety of the cage. I open the door. I step out. I walk down the corridor. I see no one I know...
T.S.	Mewa Singh waits in the witness room.
HOPKINSON	I stop at the witness room.
T.S.	Mewa Singh steps out of the witness room. In each hand he carries a gun.

HOPKINSON   When I see him, I feel myself bursting. My toy
town is destroyed in an instant. He is large, he
encompasses my world, I feel myself racing
towards eternity...They say I grapple with him. I
do not. I open my arms, I say: Now!
Dazzles the sparkle of his sword
Who is utterly dreadful and is contained not
By the elements. And when he performeth
His death-dance, how dolefully his bells
toll and knell.
He, the four-armed one, of a lustrous hair bun,
He wieldeth the mace and the club,
And crushes the swollen head, even of death.
His auspicious tongue of blazing fire
Licketh all that is unholy.
When shrieks his horrid conch
The whole universe reverberates with its
raucous notes
How tintinnabulating are thy ankle bells,
And when thou movest, thou stampest the earth
like a quake,
And thy immense gongs strike deep resonant
notes.

T.S.   Mewa Singh fires three times. A bullet pierces
Hopkinson's heart.

> T.S. *touches* HOPKINSON *with the
> cane.* HOPKINSON's *head falls forward.*

WOMAN   Mewa Singh will be hanged by the neck till he's
dead. Mewa Singh says on the gallows : "I am a
gentle person, but gentle people must act when
injustice engulfs them. Let God judge my actions
for he sees the right and the wrong. I offer my
neck to the rope as a child opens his arms to his
mother."

> T.S. *does a soft-shoe shuffle, stops,
> looks out, raises his arms, pauses and
> makes a large but simple bow. Black.*

> *The End.*

The Perfect Piece
Monologues from Canadian Plays

Edited by Tony Hamill

***

Are you looking for the perfect audition piece? Look no further gentle reader. In this book you'll find more than 130 monologues taken from Canadian plays, some reaching back 20 years, and many more from both the established masters and the rising stars of Canadian theatre. Within these pages could be the monologue you've been searching for - the piece that will work for you. Break a leg!

***

Send for your free catalogue of 1300 Canadian plays

PLAYWRIGHTS CANADA PRESS
54 Wolseley Street, 2nd floor
Toronto, Ontario
M5T 1A5
Ph. (416) 947-0201
Fx. (416) 947-0159

Printed and bound in Canada by
Best Gagné Book Manufacturers